YOU SHOULD HAVE BEEN HERE YESTERDAY:
A GUIDE TO CULTURAL DOCUMENTATION IN MARYLAND

Edited by Elaine Eff

With Paula J. Johnson, Andrea Hammer, Carl Fleischhauer, Susan Levitas, Nicholas Spitzer, David A. Taylor, Mame Warren and Brien Williams.

The Maryland Historical Trust Press
Crownsville, Maryland

The Maryland Historical Trust Press
© 1995 by The Maryland Historical Trust Press
All rights reserved. Published 1995.
Printed in the United States of America

The Maryland Historical Trust Press
100 Community Place
Crownsville, Maryland 21032-2023

ISBN 1-878399-66-7

As an agency of the Maryland Department of Housing and
Community Development, we pledge to foster the letter and spirit of
the law for achieving equal housing opportunity in Maryland.

Parris N. Glendening　　　　　Patricia J. Payne
Governor　　　　　　　　　　　Secretary

All photos by Elaine Eff unless otherwise noted.

Library of Congress Cataloging-in-Publication Data

You should have been here yesterday :   a guide to cultural
　　documentation in Maryland / edited by Elaine Eff ; with Paula J.
　　Johnson... [et al.].
　　　　　　　　p.   cm.
　　Includes bibliographical references and index.
　　ISBN 1-878399-66-7
　　1. Culture—Documentation—Maryland—Handbooks, manuals, etc.
　2. Maryland—History—Sources—Collection and preservation-
　-Handbooks, manuals, etc.   3. Maryland—Social life and customs-
　-Sources—Collection and preservation—Handbooks, manuals, etc.
　I. Eff, Elaine, 1946-   . II. Johnson, Paula J., 1954-   .
　F180.2.Y68   1995
　306'.09752—dc20　　　　　　　　　　　95-40733
　　　　　　　　　　　　　　　　　　　　　　CIP

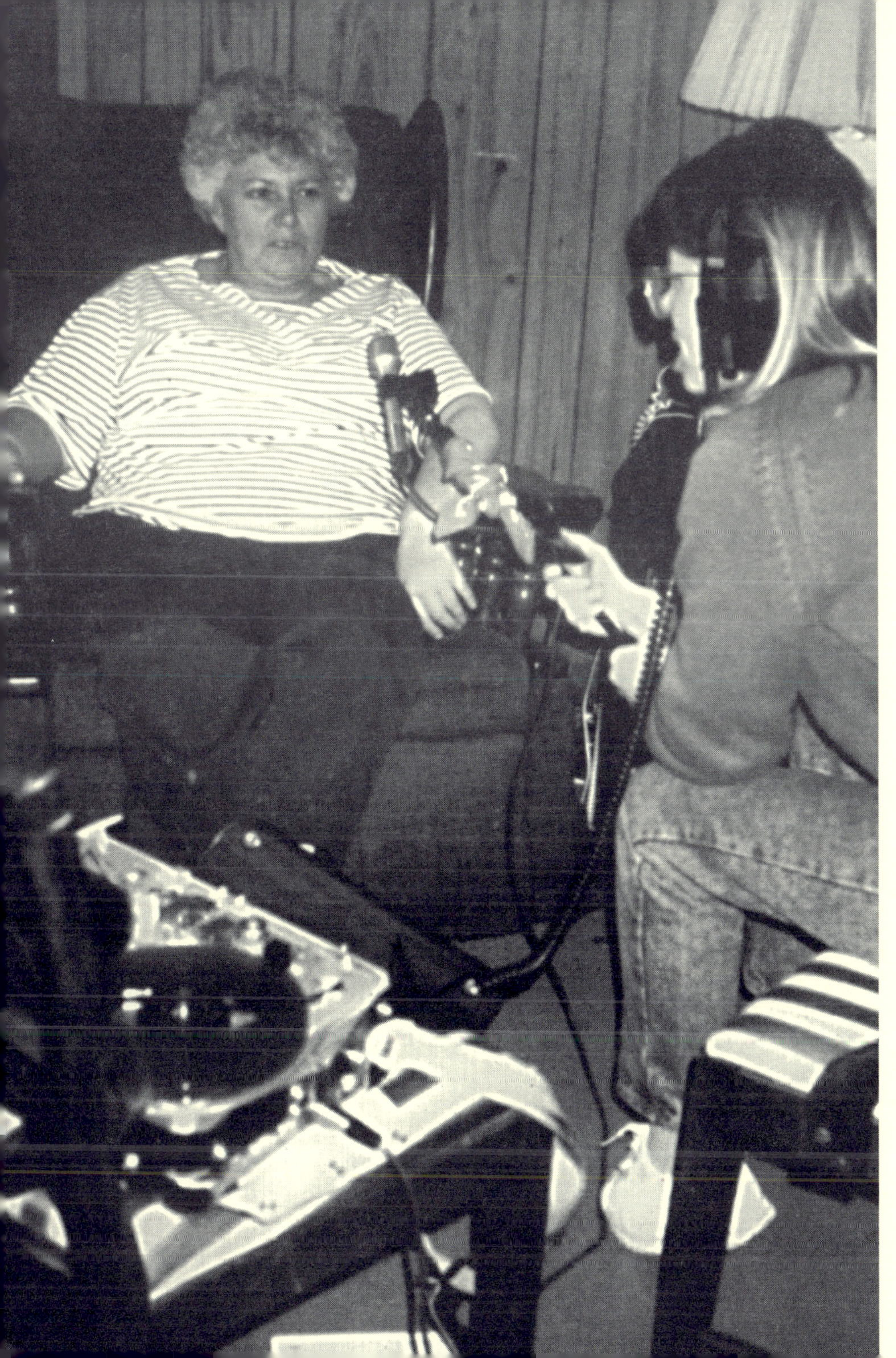

Ewell, Smith Island resident Elsie Tyler is interviewed at home with a Nagra reel-to-reel recorder and hand-held microphone borrowed from the American Folklife Center's Equipment Loan Program for a film about life on Maryland's only inhabited Chesapeake Bay island.

CONTENTS

one

WALK BEFORE YOU FLY

Planning A Cultural Documentation Project
Getting Started—Setting Goals

CHECKLIST FOR PROJECT PLANNING

CONTENTS

two

GETTING THE JOB DONE

three

FOR THE RECORD

Cover:
Smith Island men gathered daily to swap yarns around the wood stove at Roosevelt Evans' store in the 1940s. (Photograph courtesy of Maude Whitelock)

Inside Covers:
Jennings Evans prepared a map of his community to allow visitors to take a self-guided tour of the towns of Ewell and Rhodes Point, on Smith Island in the Chesapeake Bay. It is distributed at the local motel and store.

The photographer arrived in time to capture the bookkeeper at the old Atlas Radiator Co. in Baltimore. Soon after, the building was given a new facade. Today, the radiator business is gone. (Photograph by Jennifer Bishop)

INTRODUCTION

As part of a study of painted screens, a folk art unique to Baltimore, I conducted a rigorous block-by-block inventory each summer. The second year I returned to what I had previously noted as the apotheosis of screen art: a two-story Formstone-covered row house with every window and door outfitted in a full-length pastoral cottage scene painted on ancient, wood-framed screens. But no screens were visible. In fact, the house in question now sported new vinyl windows. Certain that I had made some error, I inquired of a gentleman who emerged from the house, "Am I mistaken or had there recently been spectacular screens here?" To which he replied, "You should have been here yesterday. We just threw those old things out with the trash."

"You should have been here yesterday" is the all too familiar refrain that cultural researchers hear when seeking out old-timers or artifacts. Too often we are alerted to the perfect "informant" through death notices in the local newspaper. Or we learn about a family album or work of art that went out with the attic clean-up the day before.

Only through living memory can we begin to reconstruct a past which might otherwise be forgotten. The Maryland Historical Trust, the state historic preservation office, has long recognized the value of the built environment and historic landscapes. Through the Maryland Inventory of Historic Properties and National Register of Historic Places, thousands of buildings, neighborhoods and streets have been identified, documented and protected. In 1989, the inseparable link between people, places and traditions was acknowledged with the creation of the Office of Cultural Conservation Programs. The goal is to systematically identify, document, preserve and present the traditions and knowledge that inform and illuminate the places we inhabit and use.

Shared beliefs, activities, skills and stories add a dynamic dimension to the places we know intimately or in passing. Aspects of traditional life and lore enhance our experience and understanding of the world around us. Empty lots, overgrown riverbanks or sleek highway cloverleafs may be all that remain of corner stores, factories, and neighborhoods. We can give new meaning to landmarks of another era by bringing them back to life through creative interventions and the culture of memory.

This book is a response to the numerous inquiries received at the Office of Cultural Conservation Programs. Not since the

The Painted Screen Society of Baltimore, Inc. sponsors hands-on workshops throughout the city to keep alive the unique urban folk art.

"You should have been here yesterday," when Queen Anne-style homes in Baltimore's Walbrook neighborhood occupied this now vacant lot. Not surprisingly, people forget what was once there.

The streets of West Baltimore provide a backdrop for Arabbers who continue an urban occupation unchanged over the centuries.

American Bicentennial has there been such a groundswell of public interest in aspects of regional and community life. Spokespersons for local historical societies, community organizations, trades and neighborhoods approach us regularly with the notion that they want to do something, but don't quite know what or how to begin. Because grassroots efforts are most effective when they are of, for and by the people they present, we have assembled this volume to jump-start the urge to document with proper skills and information.

There is no dearth of project ideas and no shortage of talented and resourceful people who can carry out a well-made plan. Our only fear is that the rich well of Maryland traditional knowledge will run dry as practitioners of vanishing occupations, bearers of unique skills and information pass on with no one to record or remember. It is essential as neighbors, kin and researchers that we act quickly and thoughtfully to capture thoughts and processes in permanent form.

This book is an outgrowth of two years of cultural documentation workshops held in four locations throughout the state. Seasoned professionals in the fields of folklore and oral history who have expertise in project planning and implementation, photographic and archival documents have tested the advice shared here in field and classroom situations. Over one hundred workshop participants, each with a documentation project in mind, returned home equipped with the rudiments for an action plan and a workbook which could be referred to and passed along.

By popular demand we have augmented the modest course guide in order to make it more useful and available. Our best advice is to learn well the basic skills of organization, inquiry, and presentation so that no effort is wasted— to understand from the start what makes a good research project, what themes are best suited for investigation and what kind of final product best fits the needs of the community and the subject matter. Our goal is to enable Marylanders to tell and share their own stories, to fashion and complete meaningful projects of a quality that will have lasting lessons for tomorrow.

Elaine Eff
The Maryland Historical Trust
Crownsville MD

ACKNOWLEDGMENTS

During the spring of 1993 and 1994, the Maryland Historical Trust sponsored a series of educational road shows that brought together groups of Marylanders in Chestertown, Hagerstown, La Plata and Princess Anne for a series of one-day cultural documentation workshops. Students of all ages graciously shared their visions for projects as diverse as midwifery in Calvert County, coal miners in Garrett County, and a World War II factory community in Middle River, Baltimore County.

Our dedicated faculty made the dreams of cultural documentation seem within reach. I am especially grateful to Paula Johnson, a valued colleague whose thoughtful contributions are evident throughout this volume. She and Andrea Hammer, whose love for teaching and oral history is palpable, added significantly to the workshops for two successive years. Carl Fleischhauer and Mame Warren shared their genius honed over years of acquiring and protecting photographic images. Brien Williams helped us appreciate that learning the rudiments of documentation is essential before making the giant step to video. Sharie Valerio reprised *Annapolis I Remember* from its theatrical adaptation. Folklorists Susan Levitas, David Taylor and Nick Spitzer each contributed rich perspectives gained in team and solo field experiences that culminated in innovative public programs.

At each of the four host sites, we are indebted to liaisons who lessened our burden. Members of the Trust's County Committees and Historic District Commissioners provided invaluable outreach in each region. Special thanks are due to Professor Richard Striner and Washington College in Chestertown; Susan Salvatore, and the City of Hagerstown Planning Department, the Washington County Free Library; Sarah Barley of the Southern Maryland Studies Center and Charles County Community College; Mrs. Howard F. Yerges of the Somerset County Historical Trust, and Oliver Childs, who enabled us to inaugurate the Henson Center at the University of Maryland Eastern Shore.

These workshops would not have been possible without Suzanne King, the Trust's remarkable Education Administrator who makes every detail of workshop planning seem easy and, above all, fun. Her unflagging good nature and energy brought a quality experience to residents from each county in Maryland. We are equally blessed at the Trust to have the occasional services of editor Lillian Wray, who only knows how to coax the good from any situation. That this book exists is largely due to her kindness above and beyond her job. For taking the time to plow through this manuscript when other duties beckoned, I am indebted to Lillian, Paula Johnson and to my husband John Fairhall, who says he now understands what I do for a living.

Sincere thanks are due to my assistant Bernadette Pulley-Pruitt, Development Director Donna Stupski and intern Nicole Diehlmann at the Maryland Historical Trust who provided invaluable research and support, and Brian Prince and Dave Tillman of the Department of Housing and Community Development's Office of Public Information. Dennis Towns and Tenby Owens offered insights based on their experience as sound recordist and community organizer/folkorist respectively. I feel honored and downright lucky to work once again with the immensely talented and patient graphic designer Gigi Moore who, after this project, embarks on an equally creative new career as a nurse-midwife.

Most significant is the value placed on cultural conservation by the Maryland Historical Trust and its Office of Research, Survey and Registration (ORSR). Without the continuing support of Maryland Historical Trust Director J. Rodney Little and ORSR Chief Orlando Ridout V, the voices of so many Marylanders would be lost.

Elaine Eff

Hagerstown's Western Maryland Railway yard workers proudly posed and later signed their worksite portrait. (Photographer unknown) Courtesy: Maryland State Archives (Robert G. Merrick Collection) MSA SC 1477-5982.

ELAINE EFF administers the Cultural Conservation Program for the Maryland Division of Historical and Cultural Programs, which provides technical assistance to groups and individuals planning cultural documentation projects throughout Maryland. Eff's research has culminated in surveys, films, exhibitions, articles and public programs including the award-winning documentary "The Screen Painters."

CONTRIBUTORS

PAULA JOHNSON is maritime history specialist at the National Museum of American History of the Smithsonian Institution in Washington, D.C. Her tenure as Curator and Acting Director of the Calvert Marine Museum in Solomons, Maryland yielded the book *Working the Water* and exhibitions on the history and culture of the Patuxent River region.

ANDREA HAMMER is Professor of English at St. Mary's College in Maryland where she directs the St. Mary's Documentation Center. Her oral history and cultural journalism courses have resulted in numerous books, exhibitions and recording projects including *But Now When I Look Back*.

CARL FLEISCHHAUER is a documentary photographer, filmmaker and producer of musical recordings. He directed multi-disciplinary cultural research teams for the American Folklife Center and at present oversees the American Memory project for the Library of Congress. He is the co-author of *Documenting America, 1935-1943*.

SUSAN LEVITAS is a folklorist and filmmaker whose fieldwork includes railroad heritage in Hagerstown, MD for the book *Railroad Ties* and in Cumberland, MD for the Canal Place Cultural Survey. She has conducted field projects on America's industrial cities, urban markets and inner city music in Washington, D.C. for festivals, film and publication.

NICHOLAS SPITZER served as Louisiana state folklorist for over a decade before returning to Washington, D.C. to develop cultural programming at the Smithsonian Institution. He has styled traditional music for Carnegie Hall and Wolf Trap's Folk Masters series and is a National Public Radio contributor. He is the co-editor of *Public Folklore*.

DAVID A. TAYLOR is a folklife researcher at the American Folklife Center at the Library of Congress. His book *Documenting Maritime Folklife* is the result of independent and team research projects conducted from Newfoundland to Florida.

MAME WARREN has been Curator of Photographs for the Maryland State Archives in Annapolis since 1985. Her quests for early images of the state have culminated in various volumes and exhibitions including *Then Again— Annapolis 1900-1965* and *Bringing Back the Bay*.

BRIEN WILLIAMS is an independent media producer who specializes in videography and oral history. He has worked with the Smithsonian Institution and several Washington television stations.

Despite the fact that Baltimore's Chinatown is now greatly diminished in size and population, it continues to host an annual New Year's celebration. (Photograph by Roger Echols)

one

WALK BEFORE YOU FLY

Frank Deoms, a one-time paperhanger, carney, puppeteer, and jack-of-all-trades never knew when he would find himself at work or at what. As he told it, "I would be walking down the street and I can't see any addresses on the houses, so I look at the curb and I think, uh-oh, I got myself a job." Like Frank, who passed away in his mid-eighties long after his luminescent curbside numbers faded, we too may never know when a roadside vision or the loss of a local treasure will spur us into action. In the preservation community, we are both saddened and heartened by how often we hear:

> *"Old-timers are passing on."*
> *"The neighborhood is changing."*
> *"What this town needs is a museum."*
> *"Let's do an oral history."*

A simple idea or observation is often sufficient to spur thought into enterprise — to turn a void into a job. The challenge of making a permanent record of familiar surroundings is in translating that idea into a tangible goal through a practical course of action. By moving ahead with a clear, well-thought out plan you will develop credibility for yourself, your project and the community. Whether a team member or an individual, whoever initiates or designs the project should work methodically towards crafting a single vision for all to embrace. The flaws in an overly-ambitious, ill-conceived plan will appear all too quickly. Anticipate where the strengths of your material and resources lie before determining your final product. Walk before you fly.

A young Chesapeake Bay waterman's gravemarker proudly and permanently bears the symbol of his occupation in the Ewell, Smith Island graveyard.

Distinguish between the *content* or "what it's about," and the *product*, the vehicle which gives the idea a form that can be shared. Oral history, for example, is a means to an end, not an end in itself. It should be viewed as a conversation with the past, which in turn

Charles McIntyre returns to the boarded up Shallmar Coal Company store in Garrett County where he worked as a young man.

creates documentation to be adapted to other forms. Exhibitions, films, festivals, museums, and publications are ends which require considerable labors and resources to be fully realized.

PROJECT SCOPE

Determine the boundaries of the project in terms of geography, time period to be studied, topics or themes to be explored, the community, and the audience. What may seem like obvious questions must be asked and answered at the outset to avoid conflict further ahead. Although some aspects of the project scope may change once you are underway, you should begin with certain defining limits.

A decision by the Eastern Baltimore Chamber of Commerce to examine the people and traditions of the Port of Baltimore is not as simple as it may seem. Does "the Port" mean every shipping and shipbuilding community that then and now lines the hundred mile city and county shoreline? Or only Dundalk? Locust Point? Fells Point? Canton? Curtis Bay? Baltimore Harbor? Will the study cover the history of the Port of Baltimore from its earliest days to the present, or within human memory until the introduction of containerization, when automation phased out thousands of jobs? The study then would have an ending date of 1965 and highlight the urgency of interviewing workers who may be in their seventies and eighties now.

The Mission Statement

In as brief form as possible, answer the following in reference to your project:

Who? What? When? Where? Why? How?

The importance of knowing the answers in the project's initial stages cannot be overstated. Knowing, believing and being able to articulate your goals clearly and concisely will not only help explain the vision for all involved but will benefit each subsequent stage.

Here begins the crucial process of project ownership, where mutually agreed upon assumptions are established, and upon which all subsequent decisions are based. At the earliest appropriate time, aim for a shared understanding and acceptance of the mission among all participating parties.

The simpler the mission statement, the easier it will be to gain partners at every level and every stage of project development. This written statement will become the base line for all future communication requested by funding agencies and committee members at the first meeting. When thoughtfully composed, the mission statement succinctly states your goals and justifies your organization and project.

Try a simple brainstorming session either aloud or on paper. Begin with the key terms and methods of your endeavor. Link them through a few dynamic verbs and conjunctions until you have composed a complete and concise statement. You may also find a title for your project through a similar exercise. Be careful not to get locked into a concept by a prematurely selected title. A title is not a mission statement.

Sample Mission Statements

Example 1: "Coal Talk" aims to develop a timely awareness of the fragility of a once defining regional industry and lifestyle, to generate pride in Western Maryland's coal heritage through the collection of oral histories and to create a permanent archive and collection at Garrett County Community College.

Example 2: The 20-minute documentary film "Land and Water, People and Time" will explore the daily life of Smith Island watermen and their families throughout a typical year. Aspects of disappearing island traditions will be captured in oral interviews and historic and contemporary film footage that will be featured in the Smith Island Visitor's Center due to open in the spring of 1996.

Example 3: A six-week survey of the cultural traditions of Cumberland and Allegany County will identify and document

Local resource experts like Jennings Evans are filmed to help tourists understand the lives of watermen "the other 364 days," when they are not visiting the island community.

tradition bearers from key industries and communities in audiotaped interviews, color slides and black and white prints. A finder's guide to local resources, recommendations for future programming at Canal Place and suggestions for incorporating groups and individuals in existing as well as innovative events and sites will result.

Example 4: "In My Time" is an oral history project focusing on women's lives in St. Mary's County. Interviews will be conducted with crab pickers, oyster shuckers, midwives, school teachers, judges and farmers for a booklet and theater script to be performed by students and county residents, many of whom are relatives of the original interviewees.

Example 5. The Middle River Project will present a "people's history" of the planned industrial suburbs surrounding this World War II aircraft manufacturing community. Historical research will be conducted using documentary, architectural survey, folklife and oral history methods. Residents, workers, builders and African Americans excluded for many years will be interviewed. A thematic architectural survey will examine typical buildings. Public programs will share information and methods with the community-at-large and especially with local history institutions. The entire project will be carried out as part of a collaboration with community planning efforts and the Baltimore County Office of Planning and Zoning. Findings will furnish essential data for public programming and publications in Phases Two and Three and will be deposited in responsible local and regional repositories.

Products

A clear mission statement will in turn help define your products. It is ill-advised to emulate a project seen elsewhere. Work in phases, building from discrete enterprises, which can be incorporated into a larger structure over time.

If the raw materials need to be sought, promising an extended

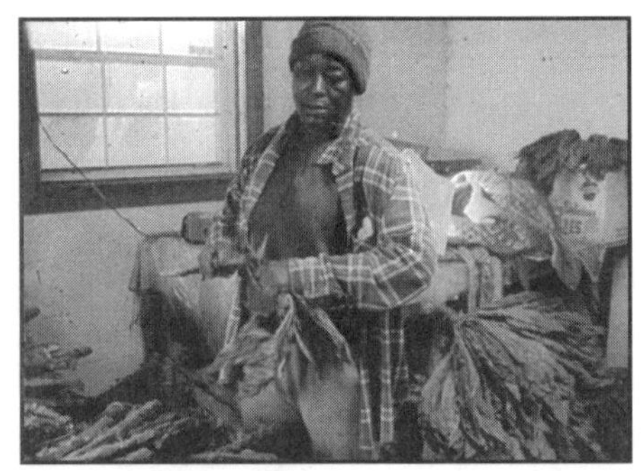

Betty Stewart "strips" tobacco at Dorman Hall's Calvert County farm. (Christopher Martin, Engineering-Science, Chartered photo for Calvert County Tobacco Culture Survey)

process, let that aspect of the project be a phase in itself, progressing to well-defined later phases. Successively refine collected materials into usable forms. Research and taped interviews with logs or transcripts may be Phase One. A book or exhibition may be a desirable Phase Two. Consider a public program, in which informants share knowledge and skills at schools, senior centers or festivals, as Phase Three. A final Phase Four might be a theatrical adaptation or a videotape which builds from the materials gathered from all of the preceding phases.

Tobacco barns of Calvert County, believed to be a diminishing resource, will be surveyed and documented in Phase I for the County Planning Department and the Maryland Historical Trust Library. Oral history transcriptions accompanied by contemporary photo documentation of the work of growers and their families during the 18-month planting, harvest, and selling cycle will be compiled as Phase II, then edited and incorporated in a report as Phase III. The report will be adapted as a book, *The Money Crop,* for county and statewide distribution in Phase IV. In a fifth and final phase, selected interviews and environments of tobacco families will be filmed and edited for a 15-minute video for use in schools and libraries.

Fit your final product(s) to the materials available. Too many would-be film producers think "film" long before they have considered whether their subject has qualities to merit a successful film. Only plan a film or video if good visuals and strong communicators are available to make the product come alive on a television or movie screen. Might a slide-tape presentation later transferred to video be a more realistic goal given limited resources?

Be careful not to predetermine your project content by choosing a catchy title that may prove inappropriate to the materials your research reveals.

A guest curator invited to organize an exhibition was given a zingy popular title by a member of the advisory committee prior to completion of a survey of a museum's rich and varied collections. Consequently, the curatorial staff was charged with finding objects to fit preordained categories rather than allow the collections to determine the best direction of the project.

Typical products for consideration as an initial phase:

Archival Materials
   These potential raw materials may result from the research phase. They enable you to move the project towards a product that can be shared with the public.

Biographical data sheet
   Oral history tape
   Raw unedited video (film) footage
   Audio tape logs
   Audio transcripts
   Historic photographs and logs
   Contemporary photographs and logs (slides and/or prints)
   Home movies (archival copies)

Publications
   Texts
   Photo essays
   Exhibition catalogs
   Recordings-CD, cassette
   Maps/ walking or driving tour guides/tapes
   Curriculum guides
   Calendars
   Posters
   Notes/postcards

Public Programs
   Museum/visitor's center
   Exhibition
   Travelling exhibition
   Touring "trunks"
   Tours (guided/self-guided)
   Radio broadcast
   Video (film)
   Festival
   Workshops
   Slide/tape show
   Narrative stages
   Oral history/theatrical production
   Photo history days
   Lectures
   Conferences, gatherings

Temporary exhibitions may be assembled from materials on hand like this "fruit crate" installation at Baltimore's Lexington Market.

An annual outdoor display at the Smithsonian's Festival of American Folklife features Baltimore Arabbers— produce vendors working from horse-drawn wagons— who sell watermelon from carts nearby.

It is important to ask what is the best medium for sharing your information. Would photographs, for example, be better viewed in a book, exhibition, video or slide show? Each option varies widely in terms of budget, labor and distribution. Will you be able to recoup some of your investment through sales or rentals?

Ask yourself whether still photographs are the best source material for an hour or half-hour video. Would live action perhaps be better suited to this format? Ken Burns' "Civil War" is a stellar example of still photographs given new life in a successful (and costly) format. Consider bringing professionals on board to guarantee a top quality product.

Oral history to be shared with the public requires articulate talkers who speak audibly, knowledgeably and in complete thoughts. Editing for sound becomes increasingly challenging when words of wisdom are found in short unconnected "sound bites" which must be pieced together electronically. It's much easier to edit interviews from tape or transcript when the final product is a book or other publication. Programs which spotlight individuals in public settings similarly require outgoing people who are comfortable with crowds. A good interview does not always translate into a strong on-stage presence.

Exhibits require compelling visuals: objects, photographs and documents. Too many exhibitions are seemingly endless panels of two-dimensional text and photographs— in effect, books spread out in a vertical format for people to walk by. And when all is said and done, no catalog, poster or other enduring form may exist. All too often, once the show is taken down, and its contents dispersed, it is soon forgotten and could only be reassembled with difficulty. This is a familiar scenario in small historical societies or on the occasion of a significant anniversary. Everyone long remembers that indeed an exhibition was held, but its donors and exact relics may never again be traced.

Audience

It is essential to know who you have in mind to receive the product as it will affect the depth and scope of the project, the choice of appropriate products and identification of potential funding sources.

When the Painted Screen Society of Baltimore, Inc., was founded in 1985 to call attention to a unique yet diminishing folk art form, its primary goal was to assure that the indigenous art maintain its place in the rowhouse neighborhoods of that city. Exhibitions, workshops and a documentary film led to television, radio, newspaper and magazine coverage which guaranteed a local audience. National and international attention followed in turn increasing local interest.

*   *   *

"Baltimore Voices" began as a bicentennial oral history collection based in six ethnic neighborhoods. Its goals were to capture disappearing stories while restoring pride in the declining city fabric. The raw material was edited into a theater piece which at first travelled throughout the six communities. Its success resulted in it becoming a jewel displayed citywide in presentations at festivals and conventions and ultimately touring as a national model to demonstrate one city's renaissance. Its format was copied throughout the United States.

"Up from the Stump"

Preliminary Research
Laying the groundwork

"You want a Smith Island 14-layer cake? I make it up from the stump. Everything real. Pure ingredients. No boxes. No cans. An authentic homemade Smith Island cake."
(Evelyn Marsh, Tylerton, Smith Island, MD)

It is unwise and often dangerous to make a project public when plans are only in the formative stage. Although the learning curve will be a high one over a short time, it is advisable to begin with your eyes open wide. Even the most superficial reconnaissance or drive-by windshield survey requires a roadmap to establish basic information before setting out. Gathering existing research as well as locating known researchers and scholars in advance will prevent you from duplicating existing efforts.

Who is the audience —

The general populace or a very specific public? Is it for the neighborhood, town, city, county, or cable television viewers?

Is this effort part of a larger anniversary celebration with planned events and deadlines?

Is the project for fourth grade social studies classes, high school history students or senior citizens?

Does the audience extend statewide or beyond? Will it interest people of a certain ethnic, occupational, regional, economic or cultural milieu?

Will film distributors, publishers or exhibition venues be able to look towards expanded sales or rental markets?

Is your goal to instill pride locally or expand awareness more widely?

Find out what has already been done in your area by visiting the library and talking to community members who have expertise in the subject of your project. This does not need to be an exhaustive search, but you are likely to learn things that will help you design your project (and that will save you from reinventing the wheel). Keep in mind the importance of network building and making friends for the project in this early period. Attempt to include people without creating more work for yourself. There is nothing more counter-productive than to be confronted by people who feel they have been left out and consequently undermine your progress. There are countless ways to include as many people as possible, from the planning stage to an advisory committee to an interview. The more people who buy into the project, the better.

Include an historian on your team if possible. In order to do competent interviews, it is essential to be aware of the names, dates, places and events important to your subject. Although your sources are considered experts in most cases, it is your job as interviewer to suggest avenues of inquiry that may not otherwise come up in the course of your interview.

Touchstones for watermen, lighthouse keepers and ocean or bayside residents include the unnamed Storm of 1933. More recently Hurricane Hazel affected thousands of Marylanders. Everyone connected with the Bay will have a story about the freeze of 1977.

Should you decide to expand upon or repackage an existing work, make every effort to develop a positive relationship with the original authors and experts. The best way to get off to the worst start is to ignore or sidestep people who have labored in the same or related subject area. When invited, they may willingly share sources, and may bless your project even if they are not willing to participate. A courtesy call to such individuals or institutions should always be among the first steps in your planning. If you are "putting old wine in new bottles" be sure that you can honestly create a solid case for your endeavor. You will not only have to convince the old guard, but you must be able to support your case to funding agencies down the road.

Avoid unanticipated roadblocks to your progress by casting a wide net based on solid preliminary research. There is nothing worse than hearing that "someone has already done it" or that you are being criticized all over town as a pretender or amateur. Prepare yourself by covering all possible bases. Remember that eventually you or your group may become the reference point, the experts on the subject in question.

RESEARCH SOURCES: LOOKING FOR LEADS

Records

Start your search in the local library or best regional library, archive or private collection. Track down local histories, maps, newspapers, interviews, photographs, census data, directories and collected clippings often filed by subject in vertical files or scrapbooks. Unpublished theses, diaries, manuscripts, deeds, home and land ownership documents and church and business records all provide the much-needed historical context that contribute to laying the groundwork for a thorough job.

Bibliography

Begin to compile a bibliography the moment you commence the project. Make it available to all project participants. Include everything relevant to your topic from books to yellowed news clippings, from film to videotaped television news segments. Keep the information on a word processor so that you or staff can keep it current as work progresses. Establish a format that will be followed throughout. It may be difficult, but see if you can track down dates and sources for those coveted articles crumbling in scrapbooks. Help yourself and others by noting where hard-to-find documents may be found. A thorough, updated bibliography allows you to move ahead easily towards a 'Suggested Reading List' for publication.

It may be equally useful, particularly if your goal is the establishment of a museum, archives or other permanent facility, to collect as many of the materials as you can, including copies of newspaper and magazine articles, films and videotapes, documents and photographs. These may ultimately form the core of a community research facility specializing in information gathered from many places but otherwise available in no other place.

Photographs of the C & O Canal as it parallels 184 miles of the Potomac river from Georgetown (D.C.) to Cumberland, MD reveal much about canal life and leisure throughout most of the 19th Century. (Courtesy of C & O Canal National Historical Park)

Retirees' breakfasts provide a perfect opportunity for fieldworkers to talk with many old-timers in a relaxed setting. (Thomas D. Carroll Photo for Canal Place Cultural Survey)

Neighbors gather at the Hatton Senior Center for a "Canton history" class to share stories of bygone trades and landmarks.

Photocopy everything you can to establish a reference file for your own project members and future researchers. In most cases, a photocopy of a newspaper article is preferable to the original in that it can withstand more handling. If you can make your copies on acid-free paper, your reference collection will have a remarkably long shelf life.

Local Experts

If you are asking the right questions, the same names will come up again and again. One name inevitably leads to another. Identify "living libraries." Ask an acknowledged local expert "who already knows it all" to take you on a tour to get the cultural and geographical lay of the land. This may involve a walk through the neighborhood, the old factory or downtown, or a car trip through the countryside to identify sites. Let the official or unofficial mayor, city manager, religious leader or other "gatekeeper" smooth your journey through town and the power structure by including him from the start. The benefits of seeing through others' eyes are incalculable.

Local experts should be considered "historians." The knowledge provided by insiders based on their years of experience will provide invaluable information and leads. You may find a houseful of newspaper clippings and documents from these sources. Whatever the subject, be sure to consult people involved in every level of endeavor—from management to assembly line to maintenance to back office. Everyone has a story to tell.

While you are compiling your information base at this stage, you are also building the much needed goodwill and community ownership that will be helpful at every subsequent stage.

Too often fieldwork is done <u>to</u> communities and not <u>with</u> communities. When planning cultural surveys, attention should be devoted to forging meaningful partnerships between people who carry on traditions, people who document those traditions, and planners, developers and government officials whose decisions can have a tremendous impact on cultural traditions. The ultimate success of efforts to conserve cultural traditions is dependent on sensitive attention to [these] partnerships.   (David Taylor)

Institutional Affiliation

At some point the advantages of joining forces with an established institution or organization may far outweigh working as an "outsider." You may wish to take advantage of specific technical or content expertise, borrow equipment, or team up for public programs, exhibition space or a storage facility for your raw data.

If you require outside funding to meet your goals, you will need to seek the shelter of an established non-profit organization in order to apply for most grants. Although you might establish your own 501(c)(3) with the IRS, you will find that most funding agencies require a minimum of three to five years of operating experience to qualify for grants. Advantages of working within a stable organizational framework may ultimately outweigh the disadvantages of the loss of independence. Choose wisely from all of the possible appropriate sponsors such as museums, libraries, preservation groups, governments, etc. Your project can gain resources such as staff assistance and credibility associated with a known and respected institution. This affiliation may also provide the answer to one of your most pressing and often asked concerns, namely the disposition of the raw materials— audio and video tapes, transcripts, field notes, photographs— generated by the project.

Network Building

From the first it will be clear that even a solo project planner/researcher cannot work in a vacuum. A project intended for public use or edification will attract contributors and detractors who cannot be ignored. Your network, tailored specifically to your undertaking, may include the community, librarians, curators, political and religious leaders, funders, museum directors, educators, archivists, local television stations, newspaper reporters, equipment suppliers and technicians. Folklorists, oral historians,

The Christmas Garden has been a Baltimore tradition for a century. Accomplished hobbyists share their memories and skills with participants of all ages in a workshop sponsored by Baltimore's Streetcar Museum, the City's Folklore office and the City Life Museums.

Documentary photographer Aaron Levin assembles firefighters at their engine house in Baltimore's Walbrook neighborhood for a survey and public programs partnered by cultural and social organizations, local government and businesses located along North Avenue.

Oral historian Barry Lanman works with students selected for a summer jobs program in West Baltimore to teach them the skills of oral history. Here they interview State Senator Troy Brailey.

videographers, photographers may offer valuable technical assistance. Common sense will dictate whose participation will best further your ends.

Teachers at every level —from elementary school to college —are often eager for an entree into the local community or to make the learning experience relevant to daily life. They may be willing to plan a semester project with your subject as focus. Are there scholars or technicians with expertise who might be eager to contribute to the project? Don't be afraid to ask because sooner or later you may be asking total strangers for money as well! Should you seek funding from the Maryland Humanities Council, you will be required to include academics whose area of interest coincides with yours but whose valuable input you had never before considered.

Whether your project originates as a bottom-up grassroots initiative, is developed by the Junior League for a local non-profit organization, or is a well funded Park Service or state program dictated by the governor, it is essential that your net be cast wide and wisely.

Advisory, Working and Support Committees

Project planning may begin when an idea is set in motion. The decision to document a cultural phenomenon may start when a single person chooses to pass along his or her vision. Once you have determined the scope of the project, your job is to sell and share that vision with an ever expanding audience. Building an appropriate planning group or committee can be a significant achievement in itself. Consider who has knowledge, influence, time, contacts and money. Be inclusive and practical. Select people who will shed positive light on you and the project and have the time and interest to make a worthwhile contribution.

Carefully consider how a committee can best serve the project. Do not create a committee for the sake of having individuals on record. People prefer to be useful, and will be alienated from the project if their talents are wasted. Develop a job description for each committee, so volunteers and staff know the exact purpose, expectations and outcomes. This information will add clarity to the process and final products.

Despite the adage that camels are horses built by committee, it is important to recognize the value of group dynamics. Too many cooks do not spoil the broth in this case, as long as a single chef is overseeing the meal. To facilitate your project, it is vital to tap appropriate supporters, advisors and workers, perhaps in three separate and overlapping groups, to help in the planning and stewardship from beginning to end. Be sure to include both paid contractors and staff and volunteers who may be involved in carrying out your plan. Unpaid committee members in particular, need regular encouragement. Keep them updated by telephone, FAX, periodic written reports or newsletters. Only when necessary, schedule meetings with written agendas so that everyone knows what is to be accomplished. Do not waste everyone's time calling public meetings to ask a changing cast of characters what they want to do.

Rather, use these opportunities to brainstorm topics and build upon available strengths to achieve consensus. Learn how people envision their community or workplace. Identify local resource experts to be visited or interviewed for contributions of knowledge, support, skill or artifacts. Be thoughtful about their time when scheduling as well as meeting. Pamper them with coffee or cold drinks and a snack as appropriate. Remember, they are doing you a significant favor by contributing their expertise. If you find they are not furthering your goals, then reconsider their individual roles and evaluate your leadership as well. There comes a time when rearranging committees only creates more confusion.

Advisory Committee

Your liaison with the professional community should be composed of content specialists as well as representatives of sponsoring institutions who in turn can brief their organizations on the project's progress. It is often useful to include an attorney as a member of the advisory committee, especially if contracts, releases, distribution agreements and deeds of gift are being negotiated. The ultimate purpose of an advisory committee is to find sympathetic, interested individuals who can donate their time to provide specific expertise and guidance among their peers. Ideally your advisory group will make inroads into fundraising and simplify working with various bureaucracies.

"Scattered in Foreign Lands: A Greek village in Baltimore" was in danger of losing a city museum's sponsorship and thus its venue for exhibition and public events despite several years of planning. A Greek-American

Frederick's Free Colored Workingman's Library was located in the front room of this home in the early 20th century. Elected representatives and community historians sought county assistance to save the building for a museum.

Candidates to consider for Advisory Committee membership:

Community resource expert
Content specialist/Local historian
Grant writer/Fundraiser (Development officer)
Attorney
Community college administrator
Union leaders
Museum curator/Director
Folklorist/Oral historian
Audio technician
Public relations specialist
Public official (from town, city or appropriate agency)
Graphic designer

aide to the Mayor with personal ties to the community intervened in his capacity as a member of the Advisory Committee to save the threatened project. His efforts also kept the village gossip network from scuttling the project at the community level.

Working Committee

Unlike the Advisory Committee, which suggests direction and policy and can steer you towards resources, the working committee produces the actual products. Their job is to uncover and assemble the information to further the project's goals. This group may be composed of any combination of volunteer and paid contractors as well as staff who may be on loan from participating organizations. There probably should be some overlap between committees to assure continuity.

Support Committee

Whatever the subject matter, be certain that the individuals or group being documented stay fully informed and stand behind the project. Consider this group your boosters, your cheerleaders. They are probably to some degree the people who go on record on tape or camera, as well as your audience farther down the road. This group constitutes your grassroots following to be tapped should you create a membership body. They must be kept current through community meetings or a periodic newsletter. The local newspaper or community weekly may find space for regular updates or a welcome excerpt from your research findings.

When Frances Kitching, the noted hostess of Smith Island, was no longer able to serve meals and accommodate guests at her inn, she realized that a major opportunity to educate visitors had ceased. A well-timed hint in the Governor's ear planted the seed for a museum. A high level Advisory Committee was created by the governor through his Secretary of State who recruited representatives of every appropriate state and county office as well as islanders and their chroniclers. This group in turn charged various representatives with the tasks of locating a site, fundraising, project development, research and interpretation and museum building. The Working Committee saw to the implementation of the project through the creation of a non-profit Alliance which ultimately became the Board of Directors for the entire project. The first meeting held on the island under the auspices of the Methodist Church/community government was attended by almost two thirds of the island's residents. The idea of a museum was introduced for the community to develop as it saw fit. This group became and continues to function as a Support Committee. Many from this group contributed their vast knowledge on film, on audio tape, by sharing family photographs and home movies and in planning meetings at every stage over several years.

Candidates to consider for Working Committee members:

    Project director
    Researcher
    Historian
    Folklorist/oral historian
    Photographer
    Videographer
    Exhibit/graphic designer
    Curator
    Fundraiser
    Student interns

Candidates to consider for Support Committee membership:

    Religious leader
    School principal
    Tourism director
    Local resource experts
    Civic/neighborhood/community leaders

Personnel

Who will be involved? What role will each person play?

What sort of expertise is lacking and where can help be found?

Will a team approach suit this project?

The answer to these questions in many cases is, "I am doing the project!" Even if you are flying solo, it is still important to have a grasp on the range of jobs that you will be performing and to touch down at every one of the required checkpoints.

Guy Hollyday worked as a college administrator, housing inspector and German and English teacher before retiring to a stone, worker's cottage in an historic mill community and beginning to study photography at the Maryland Institute College of Art. In 1986 he began photographing his neighbors. When one family announced a move to Florida, he worked with a larger goal in mind, first listening, then taking notes and finally turning to audio tape. He amassed incredible photographic studies of aging neighbors who alone held the history of Stone Hill. Then he exhibited them in stages, first at a community centennial celebration at the local library, later at a converted mill's annual art shows. At these venues, he continued to collect local stories while he played recordings as texture to his images' contexts. In 1994 he self-published the 270-page, spiral bound, *Stone Hill, The People and Their Stories*. He continues to act as publicist, hosts signing parties, coordinates distribution and delivery of the texts and has negotiated a permanent home for the tapes at the University of Baltimore Langsdale Library.

As soon as possible, you must determine whether funds are available or should be sought to hire staff. It is critical to evaluate the contribution and reliability of volunteers given increased pressures on everyone's time. Managing volunteer labor can be a full-time job. Acknowledge your own abilities and limitations and those of your committees.

Tasks should be determined and distributed early If you know you are building a museum space within a community visitor's center, bring in a consulting designer during the planning stage so that your exhibition does not end up looking like an add-on, or squeezed into the space that remains once everyone else has staked their claim for other functions.

Whether done by a single person, a team or a committee, certain tasks cannot be overlooked. Depending on the product, you have to find able workers to complete a variety of jobs.

The Team Approach

The American Folklife Center of the Library of Congress has pioneered and perfected the team approach to cultural documentation research. The National Park Service has been a visible partner in the Center's undertakings as well as in other projects like America's Industrial Heritage Project, which has supported regional teams for folklife research and heritage museum planning throughout Pennsylvania.

Community-based research projects may be best suited to short-term (several weeks or several months), intensive, coordinated, inter-disciplinary teams. Members work as individuals gathering specific information, then collaborate to compile and disseminate their findings in a single report. To date, more than a dozen successful projects have been coordinated by members of the Center's Washington D.C. staff, who design and direct each project — organizing equipment, cars, housing, local contacts and leads — to maximize team time and efforts in the field.

Topics have included buckaroos in Grouse Creek, Utah and Paradise Valley, Nevada; Italian-Americans in California; textile workers in Paterson, New Jersey; immigrant communities in Lowell, Massachusetts; and conservation and land-use planning in New Jersey's Pinelands.

Each project involved a different partnership arrangement. The Lowell Folklife Project was conducted at the request of the federally-mandated Lowell Preservation Commission to create guidelines for long-range community planning and cultural conservation efforts, and to establish a collection of archival resources for a new cultural center. Other less formal partnerships were developed between the Center and the local college, the on-site National Park Service facility, the city's cultural affairs office, and a raft of community-based ethnic organizations.

In the Pinelands Folklife Project, at the request of the Pinelands Commission and the Mid-Atlantic Regional Office of the National Park Service, the Folklife Center developed a project that surveyed the living cultural traditions of the Pinelands National Reserve and then used field

Jobs to fill:
- Project planning
- Research
- Bibliography
- Budget
- Grant writing
- Fundraising
- Publicity/newsletter
- Forms (intake, permissions, release)
- Interviews
- Record keeping
- Archivist
- Computer support
- Logging and transcription of tapes
- Architectural draftsman
- Sound recording
- Still photography
- Videography
- Exhibition design
- Layout/graphic design
- Broadcast technician
- Photo research
- Artifact collection/catalog
- Object conservation
- Curatorial
- Script/text-writing
- Editing
- Marketing
- Distribution

data to support a set of recommendations for public policy. (The project report was published as Mary Hufford's, *One Space, Many Places: Folklife and Land Use in New Jersey's Pinelands National Reserve*). In addition to the Pinelands Commission and the Park Service, other partners included the State Council on the Arts, the Historical Commission, and the Departments of Environmental Protection and Human Resources.

These research teams included folklorists, photographers, environmental psychologists, ethno-botanists, architectural historians, and labor or maritime historians to flesh out a picture of community life. Depending on the goal of the project, a team offers deeper penetration of a community, as more individuals and groups may be brought into the process.

Consultants

You may find that you cannot locate or afford long-term expertise and may need short-term guidance at critical junctures. As needed, a consultant may offer advice on whatever subject your personnel or topic dictates. Consultants may be brought on board at any time for any reason. They may be paid or volunteer their services. Humanities funders require the use of consultants to ensure the highest academic standards. If individuals with special knowledge are not members of your working or advisory committees, call upon committee members to help identify individuals for a timely infusion of knowledge.

Researcher

Ask what it is you don't know and what you need to know to assure comprehensive coverage. Admit that the expertise you seek is lacking within your immediate community and that it may be necessary to raise funds to hire a cultural researcher or project designer to get you started, complete the research phase or organize your volunteers more efficiently. An increasing number of independent "folklorists-for-hire," "freelance researchers" and ethnographers can be found plying the back roads of our state on contract to state agencies, non-profit cultural organizations or federal offices.

It may not always be clear what specialty is required to suit your research needs. Whether your project would be best served by a folklorist, historian, oral historian, maritime or labor historian, sociologist, anthropologist, underwater archeologist, Spanish language speaker or

Baltimore's Lexington Market, established in 1782, is the oldest continuous operating market in the U.S.

School groups tour Lexington Market with a retired greengrocer who leased a produce stand there for decades.

Researchers "take the lines" off a Smith Island workboat. Their measured drawings will be available to boatbuilders, researchers and hobbyists at the Smithsonian Institution.

other expert, will be determined in large part by your project goals. Let your Advisory Committee help determine the best disciplinary fit as well as select the most appropriate individual to get the job done.

Networking to gather resumes and recommendations is especially useful at this stage. See actual work produced and, if possible, meet personally or over the telephone with former employers or co-team members. If you have a limited amount of time to get recommendations for participants to take part in an upcoming festival, radio production or other public program, do not hire theoretical, analytical scholars who offer up methodologies rather than creative solutions. Look instead for hands-on, do-it-now, deadline-meeting, dynamic researchers-for-hire who have a proven track record.

For referrals, consult state and federal folklife, cultural conservation and humanities funding agencies, and appropriate academic departments at universities and community colleges.

Interviewer

Who should conduct oral history interviews? Are they volunteers or to be paid? Is the purpose of the project to teach the skill and art of interviewing, or to acquire usable interviews or both? Will they have the time and ability to pre-interview, log, index and/or transcribe? Will this be a student project under the aegis of an English or social studies teacher à la *Foxfire*? Will a core group of interested community members take on the task? Have you considered hiring a professional oral historian or folklorist to conduct interviews? Who will teach the novice students or neighbors? Will they teach themselves from a book by trial and error? Is technical assistance available from state or local sources?

Would men or women interviewers be better suited to the task? As Paula Johnson noted in her work with Patuxent River watermen, "When it comes to crabbing, the men know [their boats'] engines, but the women know crabcakes." Should insiders or outsiders, men or women, be used as project interviewers? While insiders offer familiarity with the community's history and traditions, they may know too much, and not ask questions about subjects they assume are common knowledge. There is something to be said for the "stranger factor" as details that might otherwise go unmentioned are volunteered for the newcomer. Consider Johnson's experience.

"Oystermen made an extra effort to explain to her the working and relative merits of various engines and rigs, while they assumed that her male counterpart knew about such things. The tables were turned, however, in the womens' domain, when watermen's wives assumed she already knew how to make crabcakes. When she asked for one woman's recipe, the reply was, "You take your crab meat, mix it up with our seasonings, and fry them up." When a male fieldworker was present several weeks later, the crabcake cook, who assumed he knew very little about cooking, provided a lengthy, richly detailed account of how crabcakes are made." ("Beyond the Boat," page 347)

Photographer

What kind of photo-documentation is sought? Documentary? Pictorial? Color slides? Black and white? Aerial? Who is equipped to take publishable, exhibition-quality photographs? Will it be necessary to contract with a photographer for the work you require? Is a local photographer willing to contribute skill, time and expertise as the project photographer? Who will be able to photograph people's precious family snapshots or documents either on site, at a central location or in his/her shop? You might consider a camera shop or an electronic supply company as one of your local resources. If volunteered, you may count this as an in-kind service towards a grant request. (See Funding.)

Videographer

If you are considering videotape, contact a local television station or the communications department or cable channel at the local community college. Your subject might interest a local or public television station producer or cameraperson. Take a quick inventory of potential videographers who live or work in your area.

Everyone gets in the act when residents of a rowhouse neighborhood are captured on film and tape for a documentary production about Baltimore's folk arts. (Photograph courtesy of The Painted Screen Society of Baltimore, Inc.)

Everything takes longer than you think it will.
(Paula Johnson)

Every project and each phase requires its own plan and schedule. The amount of time a project will take depends on a variety of factors. No two undertakings will have identical calendars just as they will not have identical results and products. Don't follow the example of the mass-produced cookie-cutter community cookbooks which have replaced one-of-a kind, homemade offerings. Packagers in the Midwest now provide well-intentioned groups with forms and deadlines in lieu of homespun creativity.

Timetables will vary depending on the amount of time and commitment a project director can contribute. If someone from outside the area, newly hired, is in a position of responsibility, he or she must factor in time to become familiar with the area.

A funder questioned a grant proposal involving a contract researcher who would be travelling back and forth from western Pennsylvania to Baltimore. The added expenses incurred in travel, food, lodging and days spent familiarizing the researcher with the community appeared to be money wasted. Ultimately, a cultural historian was hired whose family lived in the adjoining community, saving the project almost $3,000.

The scope of the project— whether you choose to work in phases, and what the anticipated products are— will affect scheduling. Often, deadlines are imposed from outside. The museum or historical society may dictate your schedule depending on dates they have available for your exhibition. Is a building being built to accommodate your exhibition? When will it be ready for your installation and how much later can a public opening be planned? When will a suitable auditorium be available for your event? Can you practically meet available dates? Is your product designed to coincide with a festival, centennial or other anniversary to be celebrated on a specific date? Books, note cards and calendars should be ready for distribution in early fall to take advantage of pre-Christmas sales and promotions. Which seasonal work cycles, holidays, regularly scheduled meetings and vacation times should be taken into consideration and avoided in your event planning?

Orthodox Jewish men burn foodstuffs left after cleansing their homes before the start of the traditional Passover holiday. This ritual occurs only for a few hours each year.

Between May and October of each year, Chesapeake Bay watermen's communities like Smith Island focus single-mindedly on *Calinectes sapidus*, the almighty blue crab. During this period, men are aboard their boats in the Bay's shallows six days a week, harvesting hard and soft crabs from crab pots, trot lines, scrapes and dip nets. When back on land, they and their families must devote their time to shedding the peeler crabs at the right moment for the market. Sunday is reserved for Church and family. This would be the prime time for documenting the process, but a less than ideal time for thorough, relaxed interviews.

On occasion your project may be jump-started or delayed depending on the schedule of contract workers or other staff. You may wish to alter your plans in order to take advantage of a researcher, interviewer or camera person's calendar.

Setting a Schedule

Consider all of the above and estimate the time needed to accomplish the project.

For planning and funding purposes you may wish to calculate tasks in terms of days or weeks spent. A running calendar will allow you and others to monitor the project in terms of meeting deadlines.

Try doing a bar graph. Across the top, place each month of your planned project. Down the side, note each individual task you plan to accomplish over the entire life of the project period. Be sure to put each task in the order that it will occur and number it. By drawing lines across the page, you can visualize how much time tasks will take and estimate where tasks and individual duties will overlap. You can also identify slack periods and plan other activities for those slots. This can be done by month for a long project, bi-weekly, or for each week.

The following sample project plan outlines the requisite days for preparing and completing a community oral history, based on a total of fifty interviews, for use in a museum exhibition now in the design stages. Most of the activities listed are required even if only one interview is conducted.

Factors to use in planning:

Travel time from your home/office to interview/round trip

Average interview lasts 1-2 hours

Time to log one hour of tape—
6 hours minimum to transcribe each one hour of tape

Time to log one contact sheet of b&w photos

Time to write field notes for one day in the field

Time to set up and copy photographs

Time to review each day's accomplishments and plan for follow-up

Pre-Interview

Preliminary research	7-10 days
Tour community, meet committee	1 day
Prepare/review/question sets	3 days
Schedule preliminary interviews	2 days

Interview

Preliminary visits with informants	
Schedule audio interviews	5 days
Interviews (taped sessions)	12 days
Log interviews (by topic)	10 days
Committee review meeting	1 day

Post-interview

Copy audio tapes (store original)	3 days
Transcription	7 days
Follow-up visits/audit transcriptions for accuracy	7-10 days
Edit final transcript	15 days

Total time required   75 days +/-

You may also consider a month by month or weekly schedule to clarify the work that must be completed.

Weeks 1-3	Preliminary research
Week 4	Pre-interview
Weeks 5-7	Interviews (10)
Weeks 6-8	Tape transcription (one week turnaround)
Weeks 7-9	Tape audit

Below is a schedule for a community documentation project which combines an architectural survey with oral history and public programs allowing all project participants to see the big picture.

July
Documentary research (5 days)
Log existing tapes (5 days)
Fieldwork (5 days)
Coordinate with community planning (1 day)
Drafting services (1 day)

August
Fieldwork (5 days)
Oral history interviews (5 days)
Documentary research (2 days)

September
Fieldwork (4 days)
Joint public meeting 1 (1 day)
Drafting services (1 day)

October
Fieldwork (4 days)
Meet with consultants (2 days)
Community history day (2 days)
Evaluation (1 day)

FUNDING AND GRANT WRITING

Once your institutional partners have been established, it will become clearer where money and labor will come from. Having developed a realistic plan for expenses and income— your budget— you are ready to find outside funding.

Sources exist at every level: Federal, State, County, Local and Private. As a gauge to understanding the enormity of the philanthropy field, consider visiting The Foundation Center. Whether you have a day or a week to dedicate to the search, you will find dozens if not hundreds of funding sources classified by state, funding category, interests of the funders, other grant recipients with similar projects, and myriad other ways of cutting up the donor's pie. On a smaller scale, *The Foundation Directory*, an annual publication of The Foundation Center, is available in offices throughout the state. The Enoch Pratt Free Library Central Branch (Baltimore) maintains good books on funding sources, as do most larger development offices or organizations with successful track records of securing grants, such as colleges and universities. (See Grant Sources in Appendix)

Maryland is fortunate to have state, county and regional Arts Councils, a state Humanities Council, a Museum Assistance Program and the Maryland Historical Trust, all of which fund cultural programs according to their very specific guidelines or initiatives. Always request current grant applications, guidelines, deadlines and a specific person to contact for additional information. Familiarize yourself with these forms as soon as you anticipate a project. Whether one or more grant cycles are available each year depends upon the individual organization. Some accept applications once a year; others may do so each time the board meets.

A consortium of State of Maryland grantors holds annual workshops in locations throughout Maryland to introduce their programs to an ever-increasing pool of applicants and to demystify the grant application process. Staff are always available to meet with potential grantees. Personal contact with grant officers is encouraged.

Should you wish to scrutinize examples of other successful grant applications, proposals to public (local, state or federal) agencies are public record and should be made available to you upon request. Ask to see proposals for projects similar to yours as an aid to developing your own grant. Consider attending open panel meetings when grants other than your own are being evaluated. Funders like to see a well-informed grant writer who understands the grant as well as the award process.

By reading the funder's materials, or talking with a grant officer, you can discern how much money you can reasonably expect to receive from a given funder. Once you are told what is a reasonable request, stay within the limitations! Even though you may need $70,000 for your project, do not be foolish enough to ask for the full amount from an agency that has told you that their limit is $20,000. Instead, look for multiple sources, and select appropriate categories from your budget for each to fund, e.g. computers from a telecommunications firm, film from a photo company.

Pursue funders who have a sympathetic interest in your subject. If you are developing a project about World War II aircraft communities, look towards the aerospace industry. About coal? Look towards the energy industries. Chesapeake Bay? Find foundations and private benefactors associated with the Bay, the environment and ecological activities. Ask yourself first, who should care about this project? Who would benefit from seeing this project go forward, and who would suffer if it or the larger subject in question were endangered?

Do not merely "shop for money" since in many cases you will be forced to fit your request to someone else's needs. Be clear that you are carrying out your own plan and doing what the grantor funds. Don't waste your time writing proposals to groups that only fund hospitals or education in Pittsburgh. If they say they do not fund films or books, look somewhere else. Always try to identify the appropriate grantmakers— foundations, companies, individual donors or governments— who have shown or expressed interest in funding projects like yours.

Think of your grant proposal as your project blueprint. The project proposal has two initial components: the introduction and the problem statement. The introduction verifies your credibility, experience and capability to accomplish this specific project. The problem statement states your reasons for undertaking this project in order to address a need. Describe your objectives in terms of change— as it relates to people and in terms of outcomes. What difference will it make whether or not you do the project? Why is it important?

Do not submit the same narrative to every funder if each asks for different information. Answer the questions laid out in their guidelines and ALWAYS submit information in the format in which it is requested. In many cases, a panel of evaluators or a board must make a determination based on your responses on the application form. Thus, it is very important to always try to make personal contact with potential funders. This reminds both funder and applicant that people—not paperwork— are responsible for philanthropy. Be prepared to answer not only nuts and bolts questions, but also if the project will continue after the grant money is exhausted, whether there are similar projects in your region, and the difference between yours and theirs. Know exactly what the grant money will be used for and how the participants will apply the program in their own community.

You may be looking for cash largely for the purchase of equipment, supplies or materials. You may be looking for donated products or services—"in-kind" contributions. Since few funders allow the purchase of larger "permanent" equipment, try locally to do "resource raising" for everything from FAX machines to Xerox paper or copiers, printing from a local newspaper or office space.

Recently an out-of-town researcher was hired for a short and intensive fieldwork project by a regional Chamber of Commerce. In order to facilitate his overnight stays, merchants affiliated with the Chamber donated motel rooms and restaurant meals to help keep his personal expenses down and to maximize his time spent with interviews and project planning. In turn the various donors of goods and services now take a greater interest in the project and can claim partnership if not ownership of the project.

Look in your own backyard before you go far afield. Many grantors will not consider an application that has no evidence of "matching funds" or "local match." They wonder why they alone should fund a project that no one in the community supports. You want to be able to "leverage" funds from donors who validate your project by seeing that it has the seal of approval and recommendations of local friends and neighbors. Governor William Donald Schaefer was famous for looking for community contributions when grants arrived on his desk for signature and for denying funding when local input was not evident.

Budget

A good project budget is essential to a successful project outcome. No matter who funds the enterprise, you will begin to incur costs as soon as the first cup of coffee is served. Base your budget on realistic costs to keep your project competitive. Writing and monitoring a budget is a tedious and time-consuming task, but it is the single most useful exercise you will carry out to organize and keep current with every aspect of project activity.

A complete budget will demonstrate all your anticipated expenses and income. This includes contributions of both cash and non-cash goods, services, technical assistance and labor from sponsors and volunteers. You must sub-divide categories of expense and income into the format requested by the funder and be prepared to justify each in a narrative description. For expense budgets, try thinking of these as personnel and non-personnel items. (See sidebar)

Income includes all known and anticipated sources of revenue that will be contributed solely to project activity. If an organization is sponsoring you and will be picking up part of the tab, you may include that as income. If a book is published, include profit from the sale of books or other goods as anticipated project income. If admission for a public event related to the project is charged, you may count that as income also.

The Great Derby roller coaster at Chesapeake Beach, c. 1900 - 1920. (Courtesy of the Chesapeake Beach Railway Museum)

CHECKLIST FOR PROJECT PLANNING

Once the documentation project is more than an idea, it is time to expand your vision using the Checklist for Project Planning which follows. Use it as a guide to set and share your priorities and move on towards realizing your goal.

CHECKLIST FOR PROJECT PLANNING

I. **GOALS** **MISSION** **STATEMENT**	1. Project topic 2. Why do this project? 3. Resulting products 4. Audience
II. **PRELIMINARY** **RESEARCH**	1. Research existing sources 2. Community members/local experts to be consulted for background 3. With whom should project be cleared? 4. Identify potential partners
III. **PERSONNEL**	1. Who will be involved? 2. What tasks will they do? 3. Any expertise lacking?

IV.
PROJECT SCOPE
	1. Define boundaries of project:
	
	  a. geographic area
	
	  b. community
	
	  c. historical period of study
	
	  d. specific topics
	
	  e. specific genres
	
	  f. duration of project

V.
DOCUMENTATION
METHODS
	1. Sound-recording
	  a. interviews
	
	  b. processes (skills)/performances
	    (public events)
	
	2. Videotaping
	  a. interviews
	
	  b. processes/performances
	
	3. Photography (original)
	  a. black & white
	
	  b. color slide
	
	4. Photography (copy originals)
	  a. black & white
	
	  b. color slide

	5. Measured drawings of large objects—buildings, boats 6. Collecting objects 7. Other
VI. **PROCESSING &** **PRESERVING** **MATERIALS**	1. Where will materials be stored? 2. How stored? 3. How processed? 4. By whom?
VII. **EQUIPMENT &** **SUPPLIES**	1. List equipment/supplies you already have and those you must acquire. **Equipment:** a. tape recorder b. microphone c. video recorder

d. camera(s)/lenses/flash

e. tripod

f. copystand/lights

g. computer/laptop/printer

h. transcribing machine

i. other equipment

Supplies:

j. audio tapes

k. video tapes

l. batteries

m. cables and adapters

n. film (various)

o. diskettes

p. archiving supplies:

extra tapes for duplicates
tape storage
photo storage
notes/log/transcript storage

<table>
<tr><td valign="top">

VIII.
TIMETABLE

</td><td valign="top">

1. Time varies, depending on:

   a. familiarity with area

   b. scope

   c. product

   e. personnel resources

   f. deadline imposed by
      outside entity

2. Fact: 6 hours transcribing
      per 1 hour interview.

3. Fact: Everything takes longer than
      you think it will.

</td></tr>
</table>

| IX.
BUDGET | 1. Consider all costs, e.g.:

  a. transportation

  b. photocopying/FAX

  c. postage

  d. telephone

  e. equipment/supplies

  f. salaries

  g. courtesy prints/tapes

  h. costs associated with product |
| X.
FUNDING | 1. Identify funding sources

2. Apply for funding

3. Locate in-kind support |

two

*Sonny Crowley may be the last
"brick striper" remaining in
Baltimore. He crafts his own
tools to ensure that the lines
"don't make the house look like
it's falling over." Although he has
taught his skill to his son, he
continues to be a one-man
operation.*

Getting the Job Done
The Cultural Documentation Process

Methods

Whether your project is driven by materials already on hand, or begins with a blank slate, your job is to determine what sort of documentation is appropriate.

About Video

Beginners should undertake audio not video documentation. Learn and perfect interview techniques with tape recording before attempting video. Audio and video are not interchangeable media, one being sound only and the latter incorporating sound and an image. Since home videos have become a staple of amateur documentation, increasing numbers of people naively consider themselves qualified to enter the movie-making business. Every rule for good audio documentation holds true for video recording with the added concerns for skillful camera work and editing of visuals. Professional assistance, and much practice or training is advised before planning a costlier video product.

Taped Interviews

Interviews are not impromptu conversations. They are carefully structured and require a great deal of preparation in advance: gathering background research materials and simultaneously identifying individuals to be interviewed. Folklorists call their subjects "informants," the people who inform us. Other terms for subjects include "interviewee," the person being interviewed, "narrator," preferred by oral historians, suggests a second-hand or outsider role; and "source" which is the term of choice of journalists. The person conducting the inquiry is the "interviewer." Whatever terms you select, be consistent. To simplify referents, the female pronoun for the informant and the male pronoun for the interviewer will appear here.

Locating Informants

Identify and locate informants through research and personal contacts. Working committees rarely form without preconceived ideas of suitable informants. The committee's first task should be to compose a list of potential informants. One name always leads to another.

Documentation Considerations:

Is the project driven by artifacts, interviews, photographs, documents?

Will you be interviewing people on audio tape or video tape or both?

Is truly archival 16mm film or reel-to-reel audio tape needed?

Will you be making sound or video recordings of work processes or community performances?

Will stereo recording be required for musical or multiple sound sources?

Will you need to take accurate measurements of objects or larger artifacts like buildings or boats?

Will you be collecting artifacts and photographs from individuals or institutions?

Will you or a professional photographer be taking record or documentary photographs— black and white negatives, color slides, or both?

There's an art to locating the kind of person you seek. Barber shops, beauty salons and clubs are havens for informal conversation and magnets for local gossip. Family celebrations, weddings and funerals provide unstructured opportunities for initial contacts with informants. In communities where old-timers hang out at the Liar's Bench and "yarnies" gather at the village store, you may need an entree to the group. Inquire after "talkers" or "storytellers" in addition to people who "worked at...," "lived through...," "have first-hand knowledge of..." certain experiences. Watermen, among other occupational groups, are famous for the tales they tell, but often defer to one renowned talker when, indeed, many are equally gifted.

Even after his untimely death, Captain Alex Kellam was universally acclaimed as the Lower Eastern Shore's best storyteller. He was a sought-after performer at state and Smithsonian Institution sponsored Folklife Festivals. Charles Kurault paid him a visit. His fame prevented others from coming forward and sharing their lore until his life-long associates were asked specifically if anyone knew Captain Kellam's yarns about local characters Captain Noe James and Lickin' Bill Bradshaw. Then the stories started to flow.

Pursue informants who tell succinct stories with beginnings, middles and ends. Beware the rambler who is just thankful for the audience. Elders frequently obsess on illness, hospitalizations and medications. Reserve these departures for off-tape conversation. For certain public programming goals you will be looking simultaneously for someone to entertain as well as instruct and enlighten. Style is important. 'Edutainment' is the current catchword in public programming.

List potential informants and what it is they have to contribute. Develop interview priorities based on age, health, knowledge and time available. Know that it is not possible to meet and interview everyone who is recommended. Be thorough and act swiftly to ensure that delays and poor planning don't leave you with only a pile of colorful obituaries!

Suggested Oral History Informants/Canal Place Project:
(in order of urgency)

James Wiggins	Age 90, Foreman, MD Glass Co. (in poor health)
Thomas Rand	Age 100, Kelly-Springfield retiree (in good health, lives with daughter)
Ella Singer	Age 60s, Cumberland Glass Co. (glass cutter, owns crystal shop)
Louise Hardy	Age 70, Celanese textile worker (winters in Florida)

Publicity

When a fieldworker, researcher or interviewer is ready to meet the community, contact local newspapers, television and radio stations. Once the project is well focused and interviewers are on board, issue a press release soliciting informants. Include local telephone contacts. (See Sample Forms in Appendix)

If the media does not respond to your announcement, call them within a day of receipt of your release. Obtain the name of a local reporter or features editor who covers a related beat. Even better, suggest that the local media do a feature about the project or about someone you are interviewing, making sure to include a plea for informants. Weekly community newspapers frequently print stories exactly as they are mailed to them. See if you can interest them in a regular column drawing upon the research or oral history collections you discover in the course of your project.

Annapolis I Remember began as a collection of stories and photographs about the city from 1900 to 1965. *The Capital* published interview segments every Sunday, educating Annapolitans about their history as remembered by friends and neighbors. This advertises the project and gained new leads to informants and photographic collections. The project culminated in a book, exhibition and theater presentation which was viewed by sell-out crowds of several thousand people over the course of a year.

Depending on how wide you cast your net, you may be surprised at the response. Be prepared however, to reply immediately. Older folks in particular do not like to be kept waiting.

Your project will begin to take on an identity as you move ahead. As you search for information, funding, or supporters you are probably ready to validate your project with letterhead stationery or at minimum business cards which you can present as you work your way through the community. Let the public know that you are associated with a known organization and that there is a way that they can find you by telephone, mail or FAX.

The "Mayor of Easterwood Park" met daily with his constituents at Miller's Deli for breakfast, 50 years after they have all moved from the neighborhood.

JESSICA PAYNE

Maryland Commission on Indian Affairs
Native American Cultural Traditions Surveyor

100 Community Place
Crownsville, Maryland 21032-2023

Tel (410) 514-7651
FAX (410) 987-4071

Business cards designed specifically for community surveys help legitimize and publicize your project.

My first interview was with an octogenarian farmer, Lyman Thomson, who amused himself, his neighbors and passing motorists by shingling the roofs of his outbuildings in landscape scenes as well as decoratively painting most fixed objects in and around the house. Upon meeting him and asking 'the usual questions,' he immediately affirmed "I know what you are, you're a folklorist!" Since I did not even know that was the case at the time, I was floored. He proceeded to volunteer the essential and fascinating stories I sought without my barely uttering a sound. I later learned that a folklore student at the nearby university was a tenant in his home.

In many cases, a single individual's knowledge, and storytelling ability may be your initial impetus for recording or filmmaking. "By myself, I'm a book," was the claim of at least one perfect informant, whose appeal was both in content and style— what she had to say and how she presented her store of information. Try to locate individuals who have first-hand information on specific topics. Ideally you will find articulate speakers who can share their knowledge in a warm and personable way, rather than reciting it as if reading from a history text. Be prepared for books, unpublished manuscripts and articles to appear from albums and drawers.

Olga Crouch, daughter of noted female lighthouse keeper Fannie Mae Salter, had prepared her memories for publication in a hundred-plus page hand-written text. A delightful, chatty, 80-year-old who lived surrounded by painted and photographic images depicting her family's life in a lighthouse, she answered almost every question with "As I say in my book..." She then hunted for the exact words as written. It took numerous attempts to get her to put "the book" down and speak from her own vivid recollections.

Leon Marsh describes a tool he uses for building skiffs during a taped interview. Note the lavalier microphone clipped to his shirt.

An ideal informant romances the English language in such a way that in the course of the interview, your prodding and approval are unnecessary. She can take a question and continue to supply fascinating insights without taking a breath. She will take control of the microphone and weave perfect accounts in one seamless, articulate web, leaving the interviewer to grin, nod and check off the subjects covered, never uttering a word. Over time you will learn to distinguish between model subjects and those who are lonely and just want someone to talk to. It is the interviewer's job to coach informants towards their best product, and to give them the confidence and comfort to make a shining effort.

Pre-interview planning

A pre-interview visit with your informant will help you plan your actual taping strategy both in terms of logistics and content. Contact each person in advance by telephone or letter with confirming telephone follow-up. It may be necessary to work through a third party to contact informants who are in ill health or who are hard of hearing.

A letter provides a good opportunity to demonstrate the legitimacy of the project by using letterhead and envelopes from the project itself or its sponsoring institution. Include a business card in this correspondence that describes the project and the purpose for the interview, as well as the use and final disposition of the information. Try to speak with potential informants to hear their voices and judge their willingness to speak in public. You may find a very animated and articulate conversationalist— or you may learn quickly that her information is limited. Whether by mail or phone, gain insights into her depth of knowledge and her ability to communicate without asking all of your questions in advance and possibly spoiling the taped session.

On the first day of filming "The Screen Painters" a documentary about a community based folk art, the film's researcher/director stood by the camera and soundmen asking questions of a longtime informant. Her first response was "You know that. I told you about that before." The cameras were rolling at a cost of several hundred dollars per minute. The chastened researcher/director decided in the future that another member of the film crew would ask questions from a prepared list. It was not enough to say, "Pretend you don't know me and that we have never talked about this before."

The pre-interview meeting can be reassuring for both parties. Visit her home beforehand to avoid getting lost and to calculate the driving time. Once inside, get a sense of where she will be most comfortable during the interview and which annoying sounds you might have to shut off to maximize audio quality. Consider relocating the dog, turning off the refrigerator and silencing the chiming or striking clock, doorbell, fish tank heater, air conditioner, fan, television, VHF radio, and telephone. A recorder with three tape heads that allows you to use headphones to hear the sound as it is coming in is especially helpful in identifying ambient noise. (See Equipment) Where will you and she sit? Does she have a favorite chair? Where is the electrical outlet? Is a space available for the tape recorder and microphone stand? Will you need batteries, an extension cord or three prong converter?

Use the pre-interview to explain the project and its goals, stages and anticipated timetable for the finished product. This meeting will give her the opportunity to consider how she might best respond in the formal interview and give her time to locate photographs, scrapbooks or documents for discussion.

Historic photos provide food for thought and discussion at a program designed to share objects from family collections.

Rather than be caught by surprise when boxes of snapshots appear while you are taping, you might ask during this first conversation if she can provide visuals that you can preview for later use. This is a fine time to complete a biographical data sheet. (See Sample Forms in Appendix) You may learn aspects of her life or relationships with other informants that will improve your questioning. It is often difficult to persuade an elderly person to meet anywhere other than her home. Try as you may to locate perfect studio conditions at a radio station or senior center, you may be hard pressed to get your informant to travel.

Preparing Question Sets

If you have done your homework, you will not need to ask the identical list of questions of any two informants. For each interview, prepare and review your outline or question sets in advance. Use them only as a guide to keep on track, and as a checklist to ensure that you have covered all of the essential material. Do not doggedly read these questions as written. Stay alert to the need for follow up questions. Be sure to ask 'open ended' questions demanding more than a 'yes' or 'no' or one fact answer. Make simple requests that elicit thoughtful answers. Use open ended questions that begin:

Why?...How?...Explain...Describe...Walk me through...Tell me about...
(See Sample Forms in Appendix)

EQUIPMENT

Audio Recorders

There are three noteworthy types of tape recorders in widespread use: reel-to-reel, analog cassette tape (which is the most commonly used today) and digital audio tape (DAT).

Reel-to-reel is still considered to be the archival standard with the longest life. State-of-the-art Nagra machines which run upwards from $5,000, are the choice of professional sound recordists. Nagras and other documentary equipment can be rented or borrowed "for appropriate projects" from the American Folklife Center at the Library of Congress in exchange for guarantees of insurance, repair and replacement if damaged and copies of your tapes for the Archive of Folk Culture. For a "Participation Request" form, contact the Equipment Loan Coordinator.

Equipment Loan Program
American Folklife Center
Library of Congress
Washington, D.C. 20540-8100
Tel: (202) 707-6590

The familiar full-size cassette or "analog" machines can be purchased from $30 and up. Mini-cassettes, because of the limitations due to their small size — internal microphone, thin tape, motor noise— should not be used. The only time their use is justified is for a quickie interview to be immediately transcribed, taped over, or kept as emergency back-up. Although cassettes are not considered appropriate for archival purposes as they may not be audible after ten or fifteen years, they can be used for "temporary archival" use when copied on reel-to-reel and rewound regularly. For such use a very fine, lightweight, portable machine is available from Marantz in the $300 range. Stay away from the small Walkman-type, cigarette-pack-sized machines, as their machinery is in such a confined space that it is difficult to override the sounds of the internal motor which sits adjacent to the recording heads. For voice recording and monitoring, select a larger model with VU meter for adjusting recording levels and visible battery levels, which can accommodate an AC adaptor as well as batteries. Select a machine which has an external microphone jack and Dolby noise reduction. Use headphones for monitoring sound levels as they are being recorded. Voice recording does very well with one sound track or mono as opposed to stereo's two sound tracks which are preferable for music recording, performance or multiple sources.

DAT, Digital Audio Tape, is a more recent and, for the moment, more costly format. Broadcasters prefer the clean, crisp sound. It has the advantage of maintaining an exact duplication without any drop off in quality when copies are made. Although DAT is rapidly becoming an industry standard, the cost is still prohibitive to most start-up projects. Questions about the shelf life of the DAT tapes have not been adequately addressed to recommend it as an archival medium. Sony has outstanding small units available for $600 and up. Interference from the recorder's motor is not an issue in the compact DAT units.

Microphones

Many less expensive machines have internal microphones, which are not recommended due to inferior sound quality. Always use an external microphone, preferably a shock mounted, hand-held type, attached to a mike stand and boom and placed just below and at an angle to your informant's chin to reduce plosive sounds (words with initial 'p' or 'b') and her consciousness of the equipment. Do not rely on table stands since placement may be limited by furniture arrangement or the lack thereof, and may attract the restless hands of your informant or the unintended jostling of a table leg. Always carry a clip-on lapel or lavalier microphone as an emergency back-up. The lavalier suffers from being so close to the informant's body that it may pick up the sound of silk or polyester shirts or a rumbling stomach! There are essentially two types of microphones, the less expensive omni-directional or dynamic mike that picks up a 360- degree sound pattern and the uni-directional or cardioid (and the finer tuned hyper-cardioid) which has a much more focused sound pattern. Hundreds of microphones are available from $29 at Radio Shack to more than $1,000 from suppliers to sound professionals for stage, recording and broadcast.

Tape Stock

Always buy the best cassettes you can. Maxell and TDK are a good choice. Do not try to save money on tapes. Chrome is the best medium. Stay away from metal tapes— over time they will grind the recorder's heads. Limit the tape length to 60 minute tape. Anything longer may break, jam or print through to the other side due to the thinness of the tape. To ensure that you do not erase a tape unintentionally, punch out the plastic tabs from the bottom of the cassette's plastic case after use.

Sources

Various electronics suppliers have catalogs of discounted equipment and knowledgeable salespersons who are eager to help over their '800' number or in person. Never buy without first discussing your needs with a professional. Before you purchase consider talking with experts at a local radio station or recording studio, sound professionals, oral historian or equipment sales specialists. A Rockville firm markets a "Bring it Back!" (the story, that is) discounted package in either mono or stereo that includes tape recorder, microphone, windscreen, cables and case for the novice interviewer. Their sales people now attend Oral History of the Mid-Atlantic Region (OHMAR) meetings and have begun to specialize in the needs of oral historians as distinct from musicians or journalists.

If photographing your informant and her surroundings or anticipating copying her photographs, check camera(s), film, batteries, flash. Be sure that you have your question sets, pen and notebook, release forms and project information, directions, road map and the telephone number where you are going. And remember the general rule of thumb for interviews: Whatever can go wrong will. So be prepared.

For more information contact:

Bradley Broadcast Sales
12401 Twinbrook Parkway
Rockville MD 20852
Tel: 1-800-732-7665

The Interview

When you arrive, on time of course, establish exactly where interviewer and informant will sit—where each of you will be comfortable, removed from any disturbances. Ideally you have brought an assistant who will work exclusively with the equipment to free you for the interview. Remember to disconnect or remove noisy interferences, take the telephone off the hook to assure that it does not ring or be prepared to stop your interview when it does ring. You might even put a "Do Not Disturb" note on the outside door. While an assistant takes care of setting up, you may use this time to examine photographs and documents, review the project goals and develop rapport with your interview subject while assuaging any fears that you or she may have. It is not unusual for the interviewer to be less at ease than the person being interviewed. There is no reason for fear on anyone's part. If you know your equipment and your mission, your confidence will be a comfort to you both. It is important to make your informant as relaxed as possible while at the same time gently telling her all the things she must not do— namely rustle papers, rock in her La-Z-Boy, play with necklaces, buttons or tie clips or the cord of the lavalier microphone.

If working alone: Unless your informant has a favorite chair or room, sit kitty-cornered from each other at the dining room table. Sit where you can maintain eye contact with your informant as well as monitor the volume on the recorder's VU meter, placed at a convenient height between the two of you. Consider this set-up especially if you have photographs or documents to discuss. You can minimize sounds of shuffling papers if you prepare a cushion of foam or cloth on the table rather than noisily lifting audiovisual aids from side tables or laps.

What happens when you arrive at the interview and find that your informant has invited a friend, sibling, or has naturally included a child or spouse? It is generally not helpful to have another voice or point of view adding to your well-planned, one-on-one conversation. You may suggest an interview with the second person later. Since this is not time to cause friction, at best you may try to advise them that only one person may speak at a time, since interruptions will cause problems later in the process when more than one voice greets the transcriber's ear. Group interviews usually stifle a speaker who is conscious of what others in the room may think. Discourage the presence of more than one interviewee whenever possible. You are diminishing the quality of the encounter and

Paula Johnson interviews Smith Island boatbuilder Leon Marsh in his shop. Noisy, windy conditions precluded recording here.

Basic equipment for oral history interviews of archival quality consists of:

Two Tape recorders (one back up)
Hand-held microphone (with windscreen)
Microphone stand, boom, shock mount
Lavalier microphone
Batteries or battery pack
AC adapter
Headphones
Cables and adapters
(to connect microphone, recorder, headphones as needed)
60-minute cassette tapes
Watch or clock (for timing)
Foam cushion or pad to absorb table vibrations on recorder

Before the Interview
Use a checklist to eliminate as many problems as possible:

Check your equipment and supplies.

Review the accompanying manuals.

Make sure that tape recorder and microphone batteries are fresh and working, that you have all necessary cables, extension cords and power packs.

Test your tape recorder, microphones and headphones before setting out. Practice recording and playback to assure that all systems are working and that you feel comfortable with the set up.

Pack a back-up microphone.

Set up the mike stand and boom for completeness.

Bring duct tape just in case you need to gerry-rig something. Inventory your tape. Anticipate recording for no longer than two hours, but bring four or five hours worth of tape should you encounter glitches or unexpected informants.

If the tape is not pre-labeled, label the first cassette "Tape 1, Side A and B" and be sure the tape is wound in the right direction.

the sound quality since, among other preparations, you have probably not brought microphones for each speaker. Keep in mind that a mono recorder has only one jack for incoming sound and that the recording pattern of a uni-directional microphone may be inadequate.

The interview begins with the interviewer recording a verbal introduction or "tag" at the start of the tape. You may do this ahead of time, but feeding the information in the presence of your informant can help to validate the effort and remind her of the importance of her participation. Include the following information:

Interviewer's name
Informant's name (spell out if necessary)
Location of interview
Date (day, month, year) of interview
Subject of interview
Name of project

"This is Elaine Eff. I am interviewing Bernadette Steinhice (S-T-E-I-N-H-I-C-E) Gesser at her home in Riviera Beach (R-I-V-I-E-R-A), Maryland, Anne Arundel County, on May 14, 1990. We are talking about her grandfather William Steinhise (S-T-E-I-N-H-I-S-E) who was keeper of Seven Foot Knoll Light for the Maryland Historical Trust Keepers and Kin Oral History Project."

You may also play back the tag to test and adjust the sound levels and to make sure your microphone is operating properly. This exercise may relax your informant and help her not be put off by the sound of her voice. You should begin with biographical questions which you can then play back if you believe this will overcome "recorder-phobia." Almost everyone objects to the sound of their own voices on a recording.

The single most important quality the interviewer brings is that of a good listener. Never assume that because the tape recorder is getting everything down, you can snooze, or think about other things. Stay alert. Your attention should be fixed on what the informant is saying, not only so that you can respond but so that you can prepare your next question or comment. Show your interest and involvement by maintaining eye contact at all times.

A good interviewer is a master of non-verbal communication. He has refined his gestures and facial expressions to an art, making his own comments unnecessary. The goal is to elicit flowing, narrative passages from the informant— not 'yes,' or 'no,' or 'just the facts, ma'am.'

Take notes throughout the interview. A small compact spiral reporter's pad or stenographer's notebook will allow you to turn pages quickly and quietly. Keep a running list of what subjects are being discussed. Reserve the bottom of the page for questions or comments to bring up next or later. If your notes are comprehensive, you may find that they duplicate the tape log. The two are distinguished by the presence of time codes in the tape log.

Once the interview has concluded, your informant will probably start to dredge up new stories. This is inevitable after stirring up the hornet's nest of memory. You must decide whether to resume— unpack and set up on the spot— or return another day.

Reporter's or stenographer's pad is ideal for logging and noting follow-up tasks as interview proceeds. (Dave Tillman photo)

Charles H. Green, age 85, of Dundalk, was the grandson of Craighill Upper Range Rear Lighthouse keeper Charles A. Green, Sr. He, his daughter and his wife agreed that he should and would be interviewed at home, but because his heart was weak, the visit should be limited to an hour. Two hours into the interview, his memory remained keen and he showed no signs of fatigue. On the contrary, since his interest and animation level were high, all agreed to let the session continue. Later, the family concurred that the interview was more successful in lifting his spirits than any of his medications.

Remember that oral history consists of a relationship between two people: the person who generously agrees to be interviewed and the interviewer. Every step of the interview process requires a consciousness of the pact that is established between these two individuals. You may be asking a person to share information that she has never uttered outside of a close circle of friends or family, or to speak about a time that brings up painful memories. Tact, respect and delicacy are always in order.

Folklorists interview butchers who demonstrate the skills handed down from father to son, at a public event in Baltimore's Lexington Market.

Hints for a successful interview:

Be on time. Do not arrive at an interview unprepared.

Do not overstay your welcome. An interview should last from one to two hours maximum. Schedule a follow-up visit if necessary.

Do not interview in a public place such as a bar or restaurant. You must insist on a quiet place with no distractions if you have any intention of using the recording, much less having it understood during transcription.

Do not interview outside or on a porch. You will pick up sounds of birds, frogs, dogs barking, children playing, traffic, airplanes, thunder, rain....

Avoid the "Let's hang out and rap" approach to interviews. This is not a bunch of friends getting together to gossip but a serious effort to isolate huge blocks of uninterrupted, focused prose. Take it seriously and convey the importance to your informant by your example.

Interview one person at a time. Groups tend to censor each other rather than stimulate thought.

Check your equipment. Listen to the playback through headphones to be sure that you are recording properly.

Ask simple questions, one at a time. Stay away from questions that invite "yes" or "no" answers.

Do not follow a verbatim list of questions. This is not a test or a race. Try to allow the discussion to flow naturally. Ask follow-up questions that enhance a subject—adding context, feeling and sensory information before going on to the next subject.

Do not be afraid of silences. Do not jump in to fill the void. Your informant, like you, may require time to organize her thoughts. The less spoken by the interviewer the better.

Work on perfecting non-verbal communication, using your eyes, face and hands to signal sincere interest, agreement or confusion.

Never interrupt your informant. When she is finished, seek clarification.

I recently read a memorable transcript in which the interviewer was so moved by his informant's words that he stopped her in mid-thought to tell her "how much I appreciate what you are saying." This is the oral historian's equivalent of nails being scratched on a blackboard. It was the first really compelling story that the informant had conveyed in a long interview. Of course, her train of thought was derailed.

Do not respond verbally to your informant's remarks with "uh-huh, oh yes, really? Is that so? I know what you mean." Responses are uncalled for and can ruin an otherwise fine interview. Your informant will not think you are rude for not participating in a conversation. She understands that you are interested in her observations. You can express concern, interest and empathy in other ways.

As a general rule, leave your cultural baggage at the door. When you find that your personal philosophy conflicts with your informant's, you should stifle the urge to comment. This interview is not about you. You may tell her in advance that you may not be commenting verbally, noting that you are not even miked, since it is her words that are important.

Do not turn the machine off and on, even using the more discrete 'pause' button. It is distracting to the informant and wreaks havoc on the transcriber.

Do not tape "sensitive issues." If subjects such as moonshine, political mischief, family feuds will cause the informant to restrict future use of the tape and transcript and therefore not make it available to researchers in part or whole, <u>do</u> turn off the machine and resume recording when the subject changes.

The Contract: Release/Deed of Gift

The "Release" is the contract between informant and interviewer and sponsoring institution. You must have your interviewee's permission to make public any material that she has made available to you. The release deeds the interview, transcript and related materials with restrictions, if desired, to the project and/or depository as indicated and affirms the informant's understanding of the project's purpose and process. Explain that this is for her protection as it releases the interview for educational and research purposes in addition to the anticipated product of your immediate project. It also helps to assure a donor that material will not be used without her permission and that she is not being taken advantage of. This is the informant's opportunity to restrict the tape in whole or in

Newlyweds Dr. and Mrs. Victor Miller of Hagerstown pose with their wedding party and onlookers at a B & O Railroad caboose. (Photographer unknown) Courtesy: Maryland State Archives (Robert G. Merrick Collection). MSA SC 1477-5172

part on terms she may dictate. Upon concluding the interview, both will sign and date the Release which transfers ownership to the depository cited. Leave one signed copy with the informant or send it as soon as possible with a thank you letter and any other promised information. (See Sample Forms in Appendix)

Immediately following the interview

Make sure that all of the tapes have been properly labeled.

Write a sincere note or letter of thanks to your informant and anyone who facilitated the interview. Indicate what the next stages in your project will be.

Copy the original tape, which will not be used again except for recording the final product or original broadcast. At this point cassette copies are made from the original for all parties who have been identified by you and your advisors. Consider duplicate tapes for the following users:

1. Transcriber
2. Interviewer for logging, research
3. Informant (along with the transcript as a way of saying 'Thank you.')
4. Product developer-researcher, exhibition designer
5. Repositories: archives, library, sponsoring organization

Store the original tape in a safe, climate-controlled facility. Review your copy of the tape as soon as possible, preferably while the interview is still fresh in your mind. Remember that on some days you will do more than one interview. You should try to budget time to listen between appointments, as not to confuse your interviews. Take time to write your field notes describing the context of the interview while making recommendations for future recording sessions or programming.

At an absolute minimum, log in main topics or index the tapes in timely intervals.   Do not use the counter on your machine since no two machines have the same timing and it will be useless to other people using the logs or tapes. Instead, use a stopwatch; if using a DAT machine, its digital clock, can be trusted since it uses real elapsed time. As you log, make an alphabetical style sheet of correct spellings of names, places, events, odd words or localized usages for the convenience of the transcriber and future researchers. At the same time, jot down questions to check with your informant during the audit or editing stage. In addition, any gaps in your inquiry should be indicated here for later clarification. Develop a simple and consistent retrieval system. Give each tape its own code that reflects the vital information such as informant's name, interviewer's name, tape sequence and date. Then file your tape, notes, logs, transcript, biographical data sheet and release together in an accessible, secure location. (See Sample Forms in Appendix)

Transcription

The purpose of a verbatim transcript is to provide easy access to the content while avoiding unnecessary handling of the actual tape. A recording by itself is of little use to future researchers. Few people have the time to pore through hours of tape, not knowing whether the information they seek is included. In addition, over time the wear and tear on the cassette from constant fast forwarding and reverse will only damage the fragile medium. Despite the time and cost involved, a complete transcript with index is best. You must determine the form you wish the transcript to take: Double spacing is always preferable. Do you want manuscript style? Full page or with extra wide margins for notations? Initials, full names or abbreviations for interviewer and informant? It is important to be clear with the transcriber exactly what you want transcribed. Do you want to include false starts, 'uh', 'you know,' and words as spoken, indicate long pauses? Do you want particular voice qualities noted in the text, and so on? (See Sample Forms in Appendix)

To transcribe, factor at least six hours per hour of tape into your schedule. Include a transcribing machine with foot pedal and variable speed control in your budget, or a minimum of $85/per tape hour for professional transcription. Put this in your earliest budget and funding requests. Your work will be greatly simplified if you have access to a computer for transcribing and editing. To expedite the process, most transcribers will provide e-mail delivery, or disk and/or hard copy returned to you by overnight mail, for an additional fee. On occasion you will be able to find a skilled typist who enjoys this work, may find it a refreshing change of pace and is able to contribute transcription services as an in-kind cost. More costly transcription services associated with legal work or television or radio news are available in most cities. A number of individuals and small companies specialize in oral history and guarantee seven-day turnaround.

Label the first tape as soon as you arrive for the interview. Always have extra tapes on hand and label as needed

To locate transcribers in this region contact:

    OMHAR
    Oral History of the Mid-
    Atlantic Region
    Gallaudet College
    PO Box 2351
    Washington DC 20002

A record photo of St. Mary's County resident, Alma Gatton, who shared stories about her husband George's years with the lighthouse service, will serve as a "Thank you" for her contribution to the "Keepers and Kin" Oral History Project. (David Harp photo)

Auditing the Tape

Once the transcript is complete and copied, file it for safe-keeping, then review one copy for errors in content and form. You should listen to a duplicate tape as you simultaneously read the transcript to assure accuracy. Next, send or bring the transcript to your informant for review. Names, dates and places should be rechecked for accuracy and spelling. She may or may not understand the value of this exercise so it is usually preferable to read the transcript together. If you send the transcript, you will have to stay in touch with your informant to assure its speedy return. Based on her comments and corrections, you are ready to edit the final transcript. Because you have the computer disk in hand, it should not be necessary, barring egregious errors, to return the tape to the transcriber. Prepare a title sheet including the copyright © for the transcript and file it with the index, log, biographical data sheet, copies of photographs, documents, artifacts, and other relevant data. Once you have extracted and used the sections appropriate to your project, the tape and auxiliary materials may be made available for public research unless restricted under the terms of the Release/Deed of Gift.

Saying Thank You

I was recently interviewed on videotape by a pair of graduate students for their course project. In a matter of minutes they unexpectedly turned my small office into a maze of cables and equipment. I am not sure that they even told me in advance that the interview was not a preliminary one and that recording was in video, not audio tape. The interviewer's questions were direct and precise. She never uttered a word, but glowed with satisfaction at the rich strike of information. I was fascinated to be on the other end of the recording process with such a competent interviewer. Upon completion, she handed me a release form which, in effect, granted use of the interview "forever for the consideration of one dollar." I was aghast at both the gesture and the release and sent them home to rewrite the release. When a thank you note arrived with a new equally offensive release and crisp dollar bill, I was actually insulted.

Nothing is more important than properly and politely thanking your informant for allowing you to disrupt her life for a few hours while sharing personal revelations with you. A sincere note of thanks accompanied by a token of appreciation, a souvenir of the meeting, such as a photograph or copy of the tape and transcript, goes a long way.

When the product is complete, be sure to send a copy of the publication or invite her to any public reception. Before completing a film, an interim preview of the work in progress should acknowledge all informants and local resource experts, not only as a courtesy, but in order to check your work for accuracy.

David Taylor relates a story of a group of Florida fisherman who were filmed catching a turtle in their net. During the preview of the rough cut they asked that the scene be cut due to ecological conflict. The editor was unaware of the issue. He agreed to cut the scene since it was not central to the content and he had no footage showing the turtle's release and swimming off.

Is it History or is it Memorex?

Oral history is invaluable; often it is the only source available. But bear in mind that the culture of memory must work hand in glove with the historical record. The human mind is not infallible. Facts over time may fade or be embellished. History provides a framework for authenticating oral sources. Verification is as much a part of the oral history process as labelling the tape on which it is recorded. The burden of proof is on researchers, interviewers and end users. Together, first-hand experience and thorough research strengthen the link between past and present.

Many people mistakenly think that a good oral history interview is a dialogue between two people. Neither should it be confused with a radio or television talk show where back and forth banter requires the straight man and a foil. Rather it is a directed conversation about a specific time, place or event. Consider that your goal is to bring the human voice to bear on the written record in an extended, moderately interrupted taped memoir. A series of interviews with different people will yield multiple perspectives of a single event. Truth may be found somewhere amidst them all. The interviewer may bear the added burden of not only finding good informants, but determining the difference between fact and fancy.

Folklorists, historians, anthropologists, journalists and other professionals increasingly employ oral history interviews in their work. Each discipline borrows tools and techniques from the other. Try not to muddy the waters with perceived differences in the approaches taken towards cultural documentation.

A bus transfer, safeguarded for over sixty-years, was a treasured object to one city resident

Father and son review stacks of photographs at an event to evoke the past of Maryland's oldest public market.

Photographs and Documents

The search for supporting and "stand alone" visual materials is an avenue for research limited only by your imagination, ability to travel, and photographic budget. They are invaluable as research tools when collected and archived, for use in calendars, as postcards, publications and media productions and exhibitions. Often a community's most conscientious caretakers are its longtime residents, whose scrapbooks and attics hold never-before-seen treasures. An inquiry among collectors and family members who are noted for retaining historical materials promises a rich yield.

Professional photographers, past and present, who worked in your area may provide images. The local grapevine and well-placed queries for images in newsletters of local clubs and institutions will further your quest once you have exhausted the obvious cultural institutions in the region, state and Washington, D.C. Remember that you will be asked to pay a set fee to copy and use images owned by public and private institutions.

When working with people's photographs, you must be entirely trustworthy and guarantee that no harm will come to their treasures. Carry a pair of clean thin white cotton gloves for handling prints and negatives. The ideal plan is to have equipment with you. To copy precious photographs on the spot, carry a copy stand or tripod, lights adjusted for your black and white or color film, and a large-format view camera, which assures a better, larger negative than a 35mm camera. If you do not have access to a large-format camera, 35 mm film will do just fine. Even though each copy you make after the original loses quality, it is better to have the copy than not. Unless mishandled, copying does not compromise the quality of the original. Consider inviting a local photographer who is well suited to on-site work to contribute his services.

Ask a local institution to host Photo History Day(s) as a public event to supplement your door-to-door scrapbook search. Community leaders at the library, historical society, museum, senior center or religious hall might gladly offer their facilities for a day or weekend when an invitation can be extended to all community members to share their family albums and assorted collections. Not only does this occasion provide a venue for neighbors and strangers alike to share the community heritage but you can build confidence in your project as contributors see that your goal is to build a permanent record rather than take possession of their valuables. Assure that a knowledgeable photographer is on hand to photograph their originals. Bring a piece of non-glare glass to flatten the image and keep its curling or torn edges in place.

Include an assistant to number and log each image. Take advantage of the opportunity to discuss the subjects and contents of each photograph while preparing a permanent record to accompany each photo. Create a numbering system and place it on both the Photo Intake Sheet and the photograph. Use the number to match the photo with the data sheet. Removable press-on numbers are available at photographic or office supply stores. (See Sample Forms in Appendix)

Equipment needed for on-site copying of photographs:

Large format camera
(35mm camera)
Batteries
Micro or macro lens or copy lens
Copystand or
Light stand
Tripod
Film (black and white tungsten or color slide)
Pair of lights (tungsten balanced, halogen or photo flood)
8 1/2 X 11 inch or larger sheet of non-glare glass to flatten photo
Lightweight white cotton gloves
Photo Intake Sheet
Pencil

Many of the photographs that surface may be copies that have been circulating in the community for decades. If you wish to publish or exhibit these images, you should make every effort to locate the source of the original. This will help avoid conflict over ownership and rights. On occasion, the owner may know who took the original image and where it is now housed. More likely you will have to work through established photographic collections whose curators will provide expert advice. (See Research Sources in Appendix)

As you attempt to identify photographs that are from professional studios active during the last century or before, use city directories to help pinpoint where and when a studio was located in your area or when the photographer moved from the area or died.

A volunteer logs photographs brought by Smith Islander Eddie Evans before copies are made during a Photo History Day held in a church basement.

Artifacts

While working with the residents of Smith Island to develop their "museum," it was important to understand <u>their</u> definition of a museum—a secure building, based on the historic model, where treasured objects are displayed in protective cases. Islanders volunteered artifacts they valued: grandmother's wedding dress and shoes, Indian projectile points and the last red fox killed in the nearby marsh. Three hunters each claimed to have the last red fox!

Ukrainian egg painter John Rad surrounds himself in his Highlandtown living room with design motifs from his homeland.

The most unusual items come out of boxes and trunks. Objects are useful to illustrate an informant's conversation, can serve as touchstones for exhibitions and make instructive photographs in publications. It is important to carry a camera to interviews in order to document, for the record, the artifacts that are being discussed. A photographer can be dispatched later to take studio-quality images.

Remember to measure and describe artifacts as they are discovered or introduced by an informant. Create a log sheet for artifacts or include notes on the biographical data sheet in the appropriate section. Authenticate and date items whenever possible. (See Sample Forms in Appendix)

Ask yourself if it is necessary to take possession of artifacts when they are offered, or if they can remain with your informant for safekeeping until you need them for exhibition or other purposes. Unless you work with a museum or other institution that can give an artifact a secure home and has a collection policy consistent with the item offered, leave the object as you found it. Just document it. If appropriate, suggest conservation methods or personnel. Be certain that you have communicated the importance of proper storage—removed from hot attics or damp basements.

Henry Berge's stone works was one of many located near the Baltimore Cemetery.   His sons and niece refer to Berge's pattern books and ledgers and completed works to help identify his products.

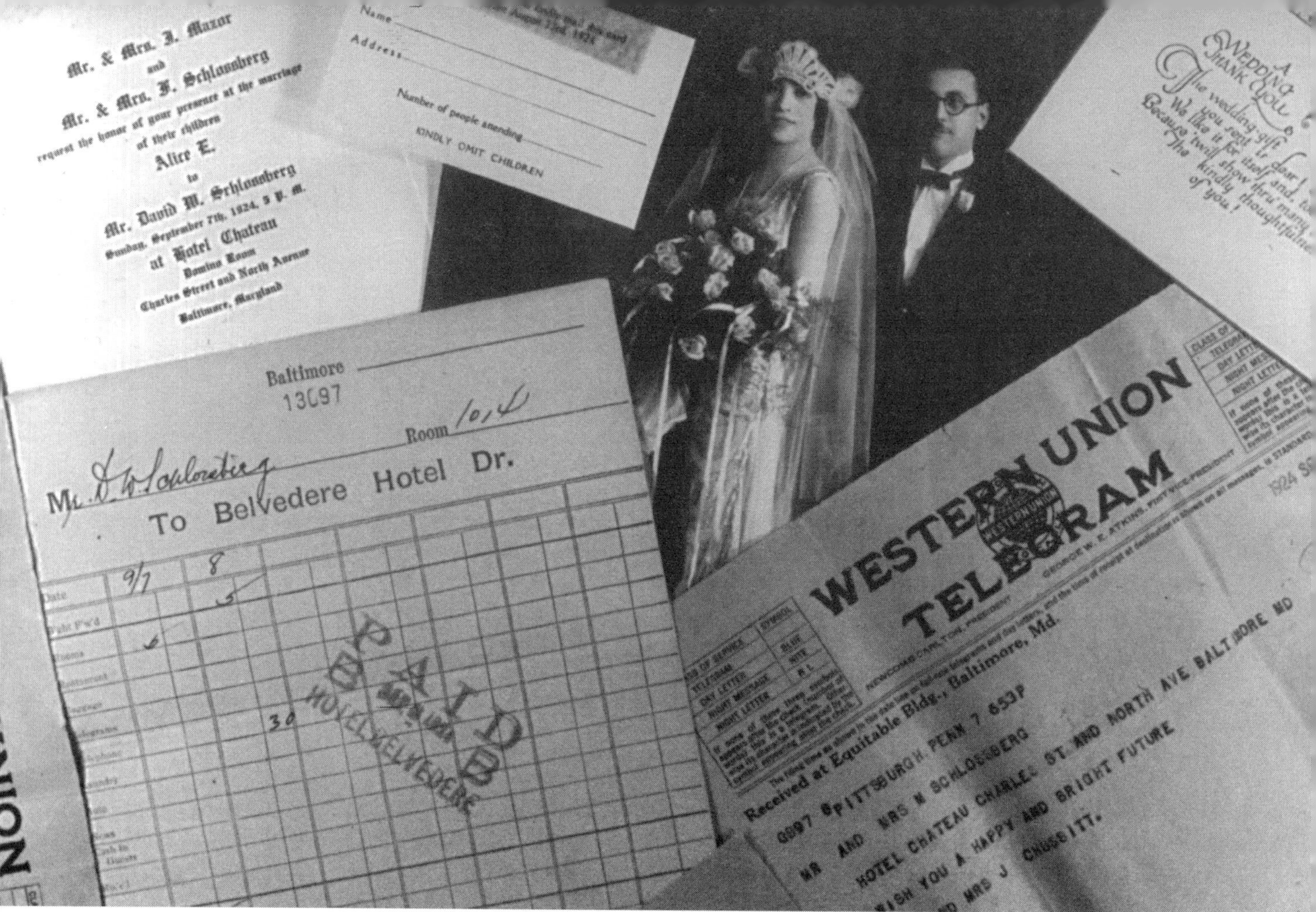

A 1924 bride saved the ephemera of her wedding day to be appreciated and exhibited well into the 1990s.

three

FOR THE RECORD

PROCESSING AND PRESERVATION

Researchers often consider their work done when they have amassed the requisite interview tapes and associated paperwork, photographs, documents and artifacts. Once the materials have been labeled, logged and delivered, this may be where the researcher's obligation ends. Then it becomes the task of the project staff or sponsoring institution to organize an intake system and render the materials useful to others.

To truly accomplish your documentation goal, these raw materials must be assured an orderly, secure and permanent home for the use of project staff and researchers who follow. It would be irresponsible to breach the trust of all who have contributed to the project thus far by allowing the fruits of your labor to gather dust in a shoebox. Ask yourself: How will your tapes, photographs, notes, and drawings be processed for long-term use? Where and how will the materials be stored? Who will do this work?

Include the cost of storage equipment and supplies in your project planning. Copy transcripts, logs and indexes on acid-free paper. Can your library provide shelves, a case or locked storage area dedicated to audio or video tapes or restricted transcripts? Electronic tapes ideally should be able to breathe where they are stored. Most equipment designed for tape storage allows for air flow between tapes. Always use a hard plastic case to protect cassette tapes and minimize dust collection. Keep tapes away from magnets in any form. Video tapes should be stored on end, never flat. Experts recommend that tape be played through at normal speed (not fast forward) at least once a year to prevent signals from bleeding through. Few operations have the staff to provide this time-consuming service.

Many archives in the past considered the transcript as the primary document and disposed of the tape. Valuable recordings which contain the voices of America's great jazz musicians, their lilting and gruff musical voices, went out with Rutgers' University's garbage in the 1950s. The transcripts can never duplicate the revelatory qualities of the spoken voice. In retrospect, professionals regret that these reel-to-reel tapes were not safeguarded in a vault after being copied to a tape medium for public use.

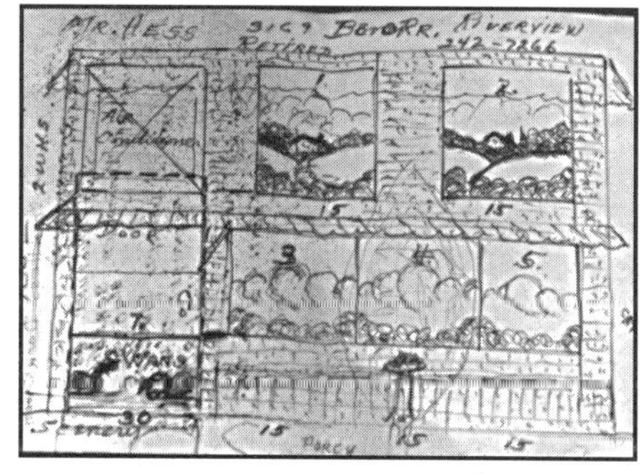

This diagram shows an artist's plan for a finished house, depicting the scenes to be painted on each of the window screens.

Snapshots copied from family albums provide valuable insight and information. Richard Oktavec, son of the inventor of screen painting, stands in front of his father's truck holding a dropcloth used in a church restoration, c. 1940. (Photograph courtesy of family of William Oktavec, Jr.)

The shelf-life of audio and video tape is a subject of constant debate given the range of storage and care options. Ideal conditions vary according to the item being stored. As a rule of thumb, however, seek a facility or container which is fireproof, has constant temperature, humidity and light, and has limited access.

Photographs present their own problems. The archival supply industry has a container for every type of image including specially designed breathable sleeves, acid-free envelopes and storage boxes .

Always use thin cotton gloves when handling photographs, negatives and slides to avoid smudging by your fingers' natural oils. This may not be the standard in most homes, but you will find it the rule in all archiving institutions.

Brace yourself for finding valuable images in home collections in every sort of array and disarray. You will likely encounter prized photo collections in magnetic page binders— the ones with the pressure sensitive stick-on pages and mylar cover sheet. Do everything in your power to discourage continued use of this format as the adhesive causes deterioration of paper and photographs. Conscientious researchers in bursts of concern have carried many an album back to the office to immediately undo damaging storage conditions. Outfitted in archival sleeves and envelopes, the precious photographs were then returned to their owners.

Because there is no industry standard, the term 'archival' must be approached with caution. A protective sleeve that is highly recommended one year may over time give off dangerous fumes and odors. Avoid adhesives on envelopes.

Photographic prints should be stored flat in polypropylene sheets sized to fit or a bit larger and placed in acid-free envelopes in an acid-free box also sized just a bit larger than the prints. Label the reverse side of the image in soft pencil with catalog numbers and other essential information. Duplicate that information and add other useful data on the folder. Avoid the use of ink pens near original photographs. Negatives may be stored in mylar binder pages in a vertical binder to ensure that pressure is on one edge only.

Mame Warren, former Curator of Photography at the Maryland State Archives suggests the following tips for preserving photographs:

DO

Store photographs in air-conditioned rooms or closets
Avoid unnecessary exposure of photographs to light
Attempt to identify the format of the photograph
      Is it a tintype, daguerreotype, cyanotype, Polaroid print etc?
Keep prints, negatives and transparencies separate
Separate color images from black and white
Describe content of photograph as thoroughly as possible
Attempt to date photograph
Identify photographer if possible
Place photographs in appropriate archival protective sleeves

DO NOT

Store photographs in attics, basements or garages
Use any kind of glues or adhesive tapes on photographs
Use any kind of ink on photographs
Use albums with magnetic or self-adhesive pages
Use rubber bands, paper clips, staples, etc. on photographs
Use glassine or brown kraft envelopes for any purpose
Use rubber stamps on original photographs
Use transparent sleeves that give off any odor
Disassemble protective cases around daguerreotypes and tintypes
Remove photographs from albums

Archival suppliers

Gaylord Bros.
Archival Storage Materials Conservation Supplies
P.O. Box 4901
Syracuse, NY 13221
1-800-448-6268
1-800-428-3631 (Help line)

Light Impressions
439 Monroe Avenue
P.O. Box 940
Rochester, NY 14603-0940
1-800-828-6216

Whether you choose to follow these guidelines in whole or in part, the steps described in the preceding pages should impart the rudiments of priority setting. Indeed, there is a great deal to think about, much work to consider and many tasks to delegate. The most modest undertaking needs serious soul-searching to determine how and if it will be done right. This volume is intended, not to overwhelm the organizer, but rather to encourage thoughtful, thorough, well-planned products which will be a source of pride to the individuals involved and ultimately the entire community.

APPENDIX

SAMPLE FORMS

You will find that project organization will be greatly enhanced with systematic record keeping throughout the project's duration. Consider adapting the following sample forms as needed for your own documentation uses:

Press release
Budget
Fieldworker's intake sheet
Biographical data sheet
Historic photo I.D. form
Still photo log
Sample questions
Alphabetical style sheet
Film/video release form
Inteview transcript
Inteview index

Personalized workplaces in factories like the Atlantic Southwest Broom Co. in Baltimore can be living scrapbooks.

PRESS RELEASE
Cultural Traditions Survey in Allegany County

For immediate release
Contact:

In conjunction with the Canal Place Project, a survey of
Cumberland's rich cultural heritage is being conducted by the
Maryland Historical Trust. To date, the Canal Authority has
sponsored architectural, economic, historical and engineering
studies. It is now time to seek out the individuals and groups who
have contributed to the occupational and community traditions
that have defined the community for decades.

 A team of folklorists coordinated by the Trust's Cultural
Conservation Program hopes to identify and document numerous
aspects of life in Cumberland for presentation in future Canal
Place public programs, books or video.

If you can share skills, folk arts or traditional lore about the canal,
railroads, trolleys, glassmaking, breweries and distilleries, the
Queen City Hotel, coal mining, ethnic traditions, foodways,crafts
and more, please call 759-6419.

\# # #

<table>
<tr><td colspan="5">NEW BUDGET
2 May 31, 1995</td></tr>
<tr><th>Personnel</th><th>NPS Grant Fund</th><th colspan="2">Local Match
MHC   In-kind</th><th>Total</th></tr>
<tr><td>Project Manager ($250/day x 33 days)</td><td>8,250</td><td></td><td></td><td>8,250</td></tr>
<tr><td>Folklorist/Cultural Historian ($200/day x 28)</td><td></td><td>5,600</td><td></td><td>5,600</td></tr>
<tr><td>State Folklorist consultant</td><td>0</td><td>0</td><td>0</td><td>0</td></tr>
<tr><td>County Historian ($30.73/hr x 104)</td><td></td><td></td><td>3,196</td><td>3,196</td></tr>
<tr><td>Senior Planner ($44.59/hr x 38)</td><td></td><td></td><td>1,694</td><td>1,694</td></tr>
<tr><td>Planner ($32.13/hr x 18)</td><td></td><td></td><td>579</td><td>579</td></tr>
<tr><td>Community Conservation Planner ($30.54/hr x 8)</td><td></td><td></td><td>244</td><td>244</td></tr>
<tr><td>Drafting Manager ($34.91/hr x 50)</td><td></td><td></td><td>1,746</td><td>1,746</td></tr>
<tr><td>Transcriber ($50/hr of tape x 10)</td><td>500</td><td></td><td></td><td>750</td></tr>
<tr><td>Project Monitor ($38.54/hr x 30</td><td></td><td></td><td>1,156</td><td>1,156</td></tr>
<tr><td>Photo/Duplication
Photography
Photocopying</td><td>
310
500</td><td>
170
</td><td></td><td>
480
500</td></tr>
<tr><td>Supplies
Audio tapes (58 @ $5)
Video tapes (30 @ $5)</td><td>
290
150</td><td></td><td></td><td>
290
10</td></tr>
<tr><td>Total</td><td>10,000</td><td>5,770</td><td>8,615</td><td>24,385</td></tr>
</table>

Canal Place Survey of Traditional Culture
In Allegany County

Fieldworker's Intake Sheet

Name ________________________________ Date ____________

Address ________________________________ Follow-up Visits________

____

Telephone ________________________________ Fieldworker________

Area(s) of Knowledge ________________________________

____

History (d.o.b.) ________________________Birthplace____________

Parent's Background ________________________________

____

School/Work/Family ________________________________

Recommendations for follow-up/leads ________________________

____

Artifacts (photos, objects, artifacts, albums, tools etc.)

____

Interview Documentation
    Photography

    Audio

ORAL HISTORY PROJECT
BIOGRAPHICAL DATA SHEET

Name ————————————————————————————

Family ——————————————————————————

Address —————————————————————————

————————————————————— **Telephone** ——————————

Family ————————————— **Tribal Affiliation** ——————

Spouse ——————————————————————————

Grandparents:

Maternal —————————————————————————

Paternal —————————————————————————

Parents:

Mother ——————————————————————————

Father ——————————————————————————

Siblings —————————————————————————

Children —————————————————————————

Grandchildren ————————————————————————

Birthplace ————————————————

Previous residence

Education

Present Occupation

Work History

HISTORIC PHOTO IDENTIFICATION FORM

Location ——————————————————————

Town ——————————————————————

Subject (Describe) ————————————————

——————————————————————————

People ——————————————————————

——————————————————————————

Source ———————————————— **Date** ————

Original Format ————————————————
(i.e., postcard, negative, snapshot, professional photograph)

Photographer ————————————————

Address (aid to dating) ————————————

Identification No. (write on back of original also) ————

Accession No. ————————————————

Collection Information (Owner) ————————

Name ——————————————————————

Address ——————————————————————

———————————————— **Telephone** ————

STILL PHOTOGRAPH LOG

Accession number _______________ Name of project _______________

Fieldworker(s) _______________

Subject(s)/Event(s) _______________

Date(s) of photos _______________

Places of photos _______________

Film type _______________

Camera Type _______________

Individual negative or slide number	Description of image

Sample Question Set/Outline

St. Mary's Tobacco Project
I. The Tobacco Grower's Space: Exploring the Cultural Landscape

Sense of Place
1. Explain, as if to a stranger, just where this farm is located.
2. What are the local names for the area, farm, district. Why were these names adopted?
3. Describe the history of this area, farm, district.
4. Can you tell me any old stories about this land?
5. Describe your earliest memory of tobacco farming.

Farmsteads
1. Could you draw a map of your farm showing where fields and buildings are located? Take me on an imaginary tour?
2. Explain why the farm is set up this way. Who planned it? Has it changed much from earlier days? How did you choose the sites for the house, barns, etc?
3. Describe for me what I might see looking over the tobacco fields on a July day.
4. What is your favorite place on the farm? Why? Do you go to any special place on your property to think or take a walk?
5. In your eyes, what distinguishes your farm from other tobacco farms?

...

Courtesy of St. Mary's Documentation Center

<u>Alphabetical Style Sheet</u>

Complete this form as the taped inteview is being conducted.

Informant _OLGA CROUCH_

Accession # _LH – OC –1_

Tape _1_ **of** _1_

Interviewer _ELAINE EFF_

Date _2- 22 -90_

<u>A B C D</u>

BEAUFORT
CHERRYSTONE
BLUFF SHOAL
BURGESS

<u>E F G H</u>

FANNIE MAY
HUTCHINS
HANNIGAN
HOG ISLAND
FEISTER

<u>I J K L</u>

<u>M N O P Q</u>

MATTHEWS
OLD PLANTATION FLATS
OCRACOKE
MACKE (DR.)
O. E. WELLER

<u>R S T U</u>

SALTER
SNOW

<u>V W X Y Z</u>

WINFIELD
YORKSPIT

RELEASE FORM

I agree to be interviewed and filmed or tape recorded for the Smith Island Center Project. I understand that the tape will be used only for research, educational and promotional purposes related to the Smith Island Center and for possible incorporation in the forthcoming exhibition and accompanying film/video.

I understand that the resulting film or audio tape will become the property of the Smith Island Center and the Crisfield and Smith Island Cultural Alliance, Inc. and will be made available to project staff, islanders and consultants for research and presentation purposes.

Copies will be placed at the Smith Island Center, the Division of Historical and Cultural Programs in its Maryland Historical Trust Library and the American Folklife Center of the Library of Congress.

Signed ____

Date _____________________

Please Print

Name   ____

Address ____

____Telephone (410) ________________

Interviewer

Name____

Address ____

____

Telephone (W) ____________________________ (H) ____________________________

INTERVIEW WITH BEATRICE GOULD
Date: February 6, 1990
Location: St. Mary's County, Maryland
Inteviewer: Elaine Eff
Transcriber: Techni-type/DDR

**EE: I am vsiting with Mrs. Beatrice Goeshy Gould in St. George Island, (Piney Point), in St.
Mary's County, Maryland. We are going to talk about her life at Piney Point and Drum Point
Lights. Why don't you tell me how lighthouses came into your life.**
BG: Well, I was playing golf and my husband was on shore leave from Craighill, and I hit him in
the behind with a golf ball and he said, "That calls for a date." So we dated, and that was the
fifth of July 1930. We corresponded back and forth until December. On December 28th of
1930, I married him. But I had never seen a lighthouse, and I said, "What's that thing sitting up
there?"
He said, "Well, that's Craighill, and that's the kind of a light you're going to live on."
"Okay. All right." So then he got transferred to Drum Point, and that's where I spent my
honeymoon. To buy my engagement ring, he wrote short stories for --what was the name of
the magazine? Oh, *Saturday Evening Post*. And he bought me that engagement ring. We lived
there for a year.
EE: What was you husband's name?
BG: William
EE: His full name?
BG: William Marion Goeshy.
EE: Where did you meet him? You said you met him on the golf course?
BG: Yes.
EE: Where was that?
BG: Bayshore Park (Laughter)
EE: When you were courting, did you not know that he lived in a lighthouse?
BG: Oh, yes, yes. The first date he took me out in his boat and out to Craighill and he said,
"That's the kind of place you're going to live in." And that's okay. All right. So then he got
transferred from there. I never did live on Craighill. But he got transferred to Drum Point and
we moved to Drum Point in December and he wrote the short stories for *Saturday Evening Post*
and got my engagement ring.
    Most of the time at night he would tell me all these stories of the experiences that he'd had
on lighthouses, and he had lived or had been stationed on the lightships for years and years and
years. One time he stayed out on the lightships for nine months, and he came ashore and he
had all of his paychecks in his pocket, and he had such wobbly legs, he sat on the curb and the
police picked him up and said he was drunk. He wasn't drunk. They tested him and found out
that he wasn't drunk. He said, "Where can I go to have these checks cashed?" And they said,
"Your best bet will be the Red Cross." So he went to the Red Cross and got his checks cashed.

KEY TERMS

Archives: Permanent repository for public records, documents and documentary materials such as tape recordings, transcripts, and photographs, which are preserved and organized for use by scholars, researchers, and the general public.

Audit: Listen to completed tape while reviewing the transcript for verification of spellings, punctuation and phrasing by informant and interviewer.

Cardioid: Uni-directional, finely focused microphone recording pattern and range.

Community: In a broad sense, any group of people sharing a common identity based on occupation, region, religion, ethnicity, gender, age, political beliefs, membership in a voluntary organization, recreational interest and the like. Shared identity grows out of such things as common experience, mastery of technical skills, possession of specialized knowledge, maintenance of traditional beliefs, customs, rituals, use of a common language, adherence to standards of conduct, as well as sharing of material culture. An individual is typically a member of various communities simultaneously; how he or she chooses to identify himself or herself at any given time is context specific.

Conservation: Preservation and encouragement of community cultural life through systematic, coordinated planning, documentation and maintenance.

Context: Description of physical surroundings and circumstances in which an individual is located or where an activity occurs.

Culture: Aspects of group or individual heritage consisting of tangibles such as buildings and artifacts and intangible expressions such as belief, skill and knowledge.

DAT: Digital Audio Tape recording and storage technology which converts sound and encodes information in mathematical increments.

Documentation: The process of authenticating through observation and tangible records, which may be notes, tape recordings and transcripts, photographs, measured drawings and the like. Synonymous with fieldwork or field research.

Esoteric/Exoteric: How a community or folk group views, organizes, and expresses itself (esoteric or "insider"); how a community or folk group is viewed by people external to it (exoteric or "outsider"). This is an important concept in cultural documentation projects, since researchers are often outsiders, who are attempting to document the esoteric traditions and worldview of community members.

Ethnography: The process of documenting a group's cultural traditions.

Fieldwork: Documentation conducted in the actual living context.

Folklife: A term broadly used to mean traditional expressive culture—custom, belief, music, language, literature, dance, art, architecture, craft, ritual, technical skill, foodways, narrative, and material culture—passed on and shared within members of ethnic, occupational, familial, religious, regional, and other cultural groups.

Folklore: Often used interchangeably with "folklife," but usually refers to traditional "lore," or verbal expressions such as narrative, song, superstition, and legend.

Informant: Individual contact who is the subject of an interview and provides a researcher with information relevant to cultural inquiry. Interchangeable with interviewee, narrator, talker.

Lavalier microphone: Small, inconspicuous, omni-directional recording device which can be worn around the neck or clipped to informant's shirt or tie.

Log: Written list of topics sequentially organized by timed intervals.

Omni-directional microphone: 360-degree 'dynamic' recording device. Will pick up voice and surrounding sounds.

Mission statement: Written declaration of project goals and methods of accomplishment.

Oral history: Personal experience narratives, recollections, and memories of individuals recorded for the purpose of expanding the historical record of a place, an event, a person, or a cultural group. For people whose history was not part of the written record, oral history research is the only way to document their experiences.

Question set: Written outline or guide to interview prepared in advance for each informant. To be used as an aid to memory not read as a script.

Tradition: Culture-specific expressions, values, and materials passed on and learned within a group or community that influence an individual.

Transcription: The act of faithfully replicating in writing or electronic media the complete text of a tape-recorded interview.

Verbatim: Word for word, as spoken.

In the 1940s, "soda jerk" Ma Phillips began pulling lemon phosphates at Doc Price's Canton drugstore. The part-time job became a long-time career.

RESEARCH SOURCES

RESEARCH SOURCES IN MARYLAND

Contact County libraries and Historical Societies in addition to the following institutions for collections of photographs, documents, oral histories and special collections on subjects specific to each region.

ALLEGANY COUNTY COMMUNITY COLLEGE
P.O. Box 1695
Willow Brook Road
Cumberland 21502
(301) 724-7700, ext. 276
    Western Maryland collection
    300 Oral histories (not transcribed)

C. BURR ARTZ LIBRARY
Frederick County Public Library System
110 E. Patrick Street
Frederick 21701
(301) 694-1613
    "I Remember Frederick" radio recordings, transcribed

BALTIMORE CITY ARCHIVES
211 East Pleasant Street
Baltimore 21202
(410) 396-4861

BALTIMORE CITY LIFE MUSEUMS
Peale Museum
225 North Holliday Street
Baltimore 21202
    Photograph Collections, Maps
    A. Aubrey Bodine Photographic Collection
    Oral histories

CALVERT MARINE MUSEUM
P.O. Box 97
14150 Solomons Island Road
Solomons 20688
(410)326-2042
    Community history, seafood industry, boatbuilding

CATONSVILLE AREA LIBRARY
Catonsville Room
1100 Frederick Road
Catonsville 21228
(410) 887-0957
    Transcribed, indexed interviews

CHESAPEAKE BAY MARITIME MUSEUM
Museum Library
P.O. Box 636
St. Michaels 21663
(410) 687-4104
    Indexed interviews

ENOCH PRATT FREE LIBRARY CENTRAL BRANCH
400 Cathedral Street
Baltimore 21201
(410) 396-5468
    Maryland Room— Photographic collections and vertical files
    Non-circulating published and unpublished works, Maryland newspapers, directories, maps
    Audio-visual Department
    Transcripts for Theodore R. McKeldin-Lillie Carroll Jackson Oral History Collection on the civil rights movement in MD (1930-1960)

GARRETT COUNTY COMMUNITY COLLEGE
P.O. Box 151
Mosser Road
Mc Henry 21541
(301) 387-3003
    "Coal Talk" interviews, transcribed

GOUCHER COLLEGE
Julia Rogers Library
1021 Dulaney Valley Road
Baltimore 21204-2734
    Interviews with MD women legislators, transcribed
    Interviews with Goucher employees, restricted

HARFORD COUNTY LIBRARY
1221-A Brass Mill Road
Belcamp 21017
(410) 575-6761
    Oral history collection, transcribed

JEWISH HISTORICAL SOCIETY OF MARYLAND
15 Lloyd Street
Baltimore 21202
(410) 732-6400
    Business, family records
    Oral histories of immigration, Baltimore
    neighborhoods

LIBRARY OF CONGRESS
American Folklife Center and Archive of Folk Culture
Thomas Jefferson Building—LJ G-17
Washington D.C. 20540
(202) 707-5510

Prints and Photographs Division
James Madison Building—LM337
Washington D.C. 20540
(202) 707-6394
    Works Progress Administration (WPA) photographs
    Farm Security Administration (FSA) photographs
    Historic American Building Survey (HABS)
    Historic American Engineering Survey (HAER)

MARINER'S MUSEUM LIBRARY
    100 Museum Drive
    Newport News VA 23606-3759
    (804) 595-0369

Chesapeake Bay Research and Photographic
Collections: A. Aubrey Bodine Collection

MARYLAND HISTORICAL SOCIETY LIBRARY
201 West Monument Street
Baltimore 21201
(410) 685-3750
    Prints and Photographs
    Manuscripts
    Maps
    Oral history collections

MARYLAND HISTORICAL TRUST LIBRARY
100 Community Place
Crownsville 21032-2023
(410) 514-7600
    Architectural surveys
    Maps, Slide collection
    Audio tapes
    Video tapes
    Oral histories of Piscataway Conoy Confederacy,
    Chesapeake Bay lighthouse keepers, Smith Island

**MARYLAND STATE ARCHIVES AND HALL OF
RECORDS**
350 Rowe Boulevard
Annapolis 21401
(410) 974-3914
    County court records
    Business Records
    Maps, Newspapers
    Historic photographs

NATIONAL ARCHIVES
Pennsylvania Avenue between 7th and 9th St. NW
Washington D.C. 20308
    Photographic collections
    Lighthouse Service, Coast Guard records
    Manuscripts

NATIONAL ARCHIVES II
8601 Adelphi Road
College Park 20740-6001
    Photographs, maps, blueprints

PENNSYLVANIA STATE ARCHIVES
Division of Archives and Manuscripts
P.O. Box 1026
Harrisburg PA 17108
(717) 787-3023
    Delta Oral History Project, Cardiff MD Welsh slate
    mining community

RESEARCH CENTER FOR DELMARVA
HISTORY AND CULTURE
Salisbury State University
Power Professional Building, Room 190
Salisbury 21801
(310) 543-6000, ext. 36312
    Abstracted interviews

SOUTHERN MARYLAND STUDIES CENTER
Charles County Community College
College Library
Mitchell Road
P.O. Box 910
La Plata 20646
(410) 934-2251

TALBOT COUNTY FREE LIBRARY
Maryland Room
Easton 21601
(410) 822-1626
    Maps
    Journals
    Manuscripts
    Church, family, business and tax records

UNITED STATES NAVAL INSTITUTE
History (Reference and Preservation) Division
118 Maryland Avenue
Annapolis 21402-5035
(410) 268-6110
    Life histories, transcribed

UNIVERSITY OF BALTIMORE
Langsdale Library
Special Collections
1420 Maryland Avenue
Baltimore 21201
(410) 837-4268
    Oral Histories from Baltimore
    Neighborhood Heritage Project, Stone Hill
    WMAR TV news archive

UNIVERSITY OF MARYLAND
McKeldin Library
Archives and Manuscripts Department
College Park 20742
(301) 405-9058
    Numerous collections
Hornbake Library
(301) 405-9988
    National Public Broadcasting Archives
    Broadcast Pioneer's Library

WASHINGTON COUNTY FREE LIBRARY
Western Maryland Room
100 South Potomac Street
Hagerstown 21740
(301)739-2350

WORCESTER COUNTY LIBRARY
307 N. Washington Street
Snow Hill 21863
(410) 632-2600
    Indexes and transcribed interviews

The Blessing of the Breads is an eagerly anticipated Easter ritual and 'beauty pageant' for baked goods and embroidery at St. Michael's Ukrainian Church in East Baltimore. (Photograph by Roger Echols)

GRANT SOURCES

Grant Sources in Maryland

Donna Stupski, Development Director, Maryland Historical Trust, compiled the following list of potential funding sources for cultural documentation projects in Maryland.

Donor Research
The Foundation Center
Suite 938
1001 Connecticut Ave., N.W.
Washington, D.C.   20036
1-800-634-2953

The Enoch Pratt Library
c/o The Foundation Center Resource Room
Cathedral and Mulberry Streets
Baltimore, MD 21201

Who's Who in America (local libraries)

Who's Wealthy in America (local libraries)

The Attorney General's Report on Maryland Foundations
This is not on the shelf. Ask the librarian in the Pratt's Foundation Center Resource Room to see this publication.

Federal Grant Sources
National Endowment for the Humanities:
Humanities Projects in Museums and Historical Organizations
Humanities Projects in Libraries and Archives
Division of Fellowships and Seminars
Division of Preservation and Access
1100 Pennsylvania Avenue N.W.
Washington D.C.   20506
(202) 606-8446

National Trust for Historic Preservation
1785 Massachusetts Avenue, N.W.
Washington, D.C.   20036
(202) 673-4000

National Endowment for the Arts
Folk and Traditional Arts Program
Nancy Hanks Center
1100 Pennsylvania Avenue N.W.
Washington D.C.   20506
(202) 682-5532

State of Maryland—Sources of Funding
Maryland Humanities Council
601 N. Howard St.
Baltimore 21201-4585
(410) 625-4830

Maryland State Arts Council
Folk Arts Program
601 N. Howard St.
Baltimore 21201-4585
(410) 333-8232

Museum Assistance Program
100 Community Place
Crownsville   21032
(410) 514-7622

Non-Capital Grant Program
The Maryland Historical Trust
100 Community Place
Crownsville 21032
(410) 514-7626

Local/Regional Sources of Funding
In addition to "Special Project" grants awarded by the Maryland
State Arts Council, each county receives an additional allocation
of Arts Council funds that it awards to projects specific to each
county. Call the Maryland State Arts Council for the phone
number of your county arts organization.

Mayor's Advisory Council on Art and Culture (MACAC)
21 South Eutaw St.
Baltimore   21201
(410) 396-4575

Mid-Atlantic Arts Foundation
11 E. Chase Street
Baltimore   21202
(410) 539-6656
Supports projects, programs, apprenticeships encouraging
exchanges and partnerships among Mid-Atlantic state
residents.

"Certified Local Governments" (CLGs) also have funds that can
be awarded to cultural documentation projects. Call the
Maryland Historical Trust to ask about the CLG program and to
identify which CLG organization is specific to your project area.
Contact the CLG first and work through them to ensure that
your project is one of their top priorities.

Maryland Corporations
Alex Brown & Sons Charitable Foundation
c/o Alex Brown & Sons, Inc.
135 E. Baltimore St.
Baltimore   21202
(410) 727-1700

Baltimore Gas & Electric Foundation
P. O. Box 1475
Baltimore   21203-1475
(410) 234-7480

Bell Atlantic Contributions
One East Pratt St.
8th Floor, East Wing
Baltimore   21202
(410) 393-7454

Chase Manhattan Bank of MD
10 E. Baltimore St.
Baltimore   21202
410-576-8112

NationsBank of Maryland
66601 Rockledge Drive
Bethesda   20817
(301) 270-5000

Signet Bank
Corporate Contributions
7 St. Paul Street
Baltimore   21202-1612
(410) 21202-1612

T. Rowe Price Associates Foundation
100 East Pratt St.
Baltimore   21202
(410) 547-2000

The USF&G Foundation, Inc.
100 Light Street
Baltimore   21202
(410) 547-3752

Maryland Foundations
The following is a partial list of possible funders for your project.
Call the foundation first to obtain grant application forms,
guidelines and the current name of the foundation's contact
person with whom you should meet. Foundations require that
your proposal be submitted by a 501(c)3 organization (non-
profit) or sponsor. Try to find a non-profit sponsor in your area
who has a natural interest in the work you propose to do and
ask them to sponsor your grant application(s).

Abell Foundation
111 S. Calvert St.
Suite 2300
Baltimore   21201-6174
(410) 547-1300

Adalman Charitable Foundation
830 West 40th St., Apt. 552
Baltimore   21211
(410) 243-4562

The Baltimore Community Foundation
Two East Read Street
Ninth Floor, the Latrobe Building
Baltimore   21202
(410) 332-4171

Alvin & Fanny Blaustein Thalheimer Foundation
Blaustein Building
P. O. Box 238
Baltimore   21203
(410) 347-7000

Chesapeake Bay Trust
60 West Street
Annapolis   21401
(410) 974-2941

Community Foundation of the Eastern Shore
200 West Main Street
P. O. Box 156
Salisbury   21803
(301) 742-9911

The Jacob and Annita France Foundation
The Exchange, Suite 118
1122 Kenilworth Drive
Baltimore   21204
(410) 832-5700

Irvin Grief Foundation, Inc.
20 Blythewood Road
Baltimore   21210

Ensign C. Markland Kelly, Jr. Memorial Foundation
1406 Fidelity Building
Baltimore   21201
(410) 837-8822

Abraham and Ruth Krieger Foundation
P. O. Box 10099
Baltimore   21285
Phone unlisted

Sumner T. McKnight Foundation
401 E. Pratt Street
243 World Trade Center
Baltimore 21202
(410) 752-8727

Robert G. and Anne M. Merrick Foundation
The Exchange
1122 Kenilworth Drive, #118
Baltimore   21204
(410) 832-5700

The Joseph Meyerhoff Fund, Inc.
25 South Charles St.
Suite 2100
Baltimore   21201
(410) 727-3200

The Noxell Foundation
11050 York Road
Hunt Valley   21031-2096
(410) 785-4361

Rogers-Wilbur Foundation
P. O. Box 46
Gibson Island   21056
(410) 437-5858

Donated Products
The Loading Dock
2523 Gwynns Falls Parkway
Baltimore
410-728-3625

Surplus equipment and supplies are available to groups with
501(c)(3) status or sponsorship.

Members of Maryland's indigenous Indian tribes share their knowledge and traditions in classroom lecture demonstrations. (Photograph by Marion Warren for "The Birds Flew Off," Piscataway Oral History Project, Maryland Commission on Indian Affairs)

SUGGESTED READINGS

SUGGESTED READINGS

PUBLICATIONS ON MARYLAND SUBJECTS

Caraveli, Anna. **Scattered in Foreign Lands: A Greek Village in Baltimore.** Washington, D.C.: The National Center for Urban Ethnic Affairs, 1985.

Fleetwood, Mary Anne. **Voices from the Land. A Caroline County Memoir.** Queenstown, MD: The Queen Anne Press, 1983.

Hammer, Andrea, ed. **Praising the Bridge that Brought Me Over: One Hundred Years at Indian Head.** La Plata, MD; Charles County Community College, 1990.

_____. **In My Family's Attic: Ridge Elementary School Reconstructing Community History.** Ridge, MD: Ridge Elementary School, 1990.

_____. **But Now When I Look Back: Remembering St. Mary's County through Farm Security Administration Photographs.** St. Mary's City: St. Mary's College of Maryland, 1988.

_____. **In My Time, When I Was Coming Along.** St. Mary's City: St. Mary's College of Maryland, 1988.

Heland, Victoria. **Worcester Memories.** Snow Hill: Worcester Heritage Committee, 1984.

Hollyday, Guy. **Stone Hill: The People and Their Stories.** Baltimore: Published by the Author, 1994.

Johnson, Paula J., ed. **Working the Water: The Commercial Fisheries of Maryland's Patuxent River.** Charlottesville: The University Press of Virginia and Calvert Marine Museum, 1988.

Key, Betty Mc Keever and Larry F. Sullivan, eds. **Oral History in Maryland: A Directory.** Baltimore: Maryland Historical Society, 1981.

Levitas, Susan, ed. **Railroad Ties: Industry and Culture in Hagerstown, Maryland.** Crownsville: The Maryland Historical Trust Press, 1994.

Martin, Christopher. **Calvert County Tobacco Culture Survey: Oral History and Folklife.** Phases II and III, reports submitted by Engineering-Science, Chartered to the Calvert County Historic District Commission, May 1991 and June 1992.

McGrath, Sally and Patricia J. McGuire, eds. **The Money Crop: Tobacco Culture in Calvert County, Maryland.** Crownsville: Maryland Historical and Cultural Publications, 1992.

Papenfuse, Edward C., and Christopher N. Allan, Patricia V. Melville, Kevin Swanson, and Constance R. Neale. **A Guide to Government Records at the Maryland State Archives.** Annapolis: Maryland State Archives, 1991.

Sherwood, John. **Vanishing Maryland.** Baltimore: Johns Hopkins University Press, 1994.

Warren, Mame. **Then Again...Annapolis, 1900-1965.** Annapolis: Time Exposures Ltd., 1990.

CULTURAL DOCUMENTATION REFERENCES

Allen, Barbara, and Lynwood Montell. **From Memory to History: Using Oral Sources in Local Historical Research.** Nashville: American Association for State and Local History, 1981.

Baron, Robert and Nicholas R. Spitzer, ed. **Public Folklore.** Washington, D.C.: Smithsonian Institution Press, 1992.

Bartis, Peter. **Folklife & Fieldwork: A Layman's Introduction to Field Techniques.** Rev. and expanded ed. Publications of the American Folklife Center, No. 3. Washington, DC: Library of Congress, 1990.

Baum, Willa K. **Oral History and the Local Historical Society.** 3rd rev. ed. Nashville: American Association for State and Local History, 1987.

_____. **Transcribing and Editing Oral History.** Nashville: American Association for State and Local History, 1977.

By Myself I'm a Book: An Oral History of the Immigrant Experience in Pittsburgh. Under the direction of Ailon Shiloh. Pittsburgh: National Council of Jewish Women, American Jewish Historical Society, 1972.

Carter, Thomas and Carl Fleischhauer. **The Grouse Creek Cultural Survey: Integrating Folklife and Historic Preservation Field Research.** Publications of the American Folklife Center, No. 13. Washington, DC: Library of Congress, 1988.

Clark-Lewis, Elizabeth. **Living In-Living Out. Domestics in Washington, D.C. 1910-1940.** Washington, D.C.: Smithsonian Institution Press, 1994.

Collier, John, Jr., and Malcolm Collier. **Visual Anthropology: Photography as a Research Method.** Rev. and expanded ed. Albuquerque: University of New Mexico Press, 1986.

Eastman Kodak Company, **Conservation of Photographs.** Kodak Publication F-40. Rochester, NY: Eastman Kodak Company, 1985.

Fleischhauer, Carl. "Sound Recording and Still Photography in the Field." In **Handbook of American Folklore**, ed. Richard M. Dorson, 384-90. Bloomington: Indiana University Press, 1986.

Georges, Robert A., and Michael Owen Jones. **People Studying People: The Human Element In Fieldwork.** Berkeley and Los Angeles: University of California Press, 1980.

Goldstein, Kenneth S. **A Guide for Field Workers in Folklore.** Hatboro, PA: Folklore Associates, 1964.

Hall, Jacquelyn Dowd, James Leloudis, Robert Korstad, Mary Murphy, Lu Ann Jones, Christopher B. Daly. **Like a Family: The Making of a Southern Cotton Mill World.** Chapel Hill and London: The University of North Carolina Press, 1987.

Hufford, Mary. **Conserving Culture: A New Discourse on Heritage.** Urbana and Chicago: University of Illinois Press, 1994.

_____. **One Space, Many Places: Folklife and Land Use in New Jersey's Pinelands National Reserve.** Publications of the American Folklife Center, No. 15. Washington, DC: Library of Congress, 1986.

_____. "Telling the Landscape: Folklife Expressions and Sense of Place," in Rita Zorn Moonsammy, David Steven Cohen, and Lorraine E. Williams, eds., **Pinelands Folklife**, New Brunswick and London: Rutgers University Press, 1987.

Ives, Edward D. **The Tape-Recorded Interview: A Manual for Field Workers in Folklore and Oral History.** Knoxville: University of Tennessee Press, 1980.

Jackson, Bruce. **Fieldwork.** Urbana and Chicago: University of Illinois Press, 1987.

Jansen, William Hugh. "The Esoteric-Exoteric Factor," in **Fabula: Journal of Folktale Studies**, 1 (1959), 205-211. Reprinted in Alan Dundes, ed., **The Study of Folklore**, Englewood Cliffs, NJ: Prentice-Hall, 43-51, 1965.

Johnson, Paula, J. and David A. Taylor. "Beyond the Boat: Documenting the Cultural Context," in Paul Lipke, Peter Spectre, and Benjamin A.G. Fuller, **Boats. A Manual for Their Documentation**. Nashville: American Association for State and Local History, 1993.

Kammen, Carol. **On Doing Local History: Reflections on What Local Historians Do, Why, and What it Means.** Nashville: American Association for State and Local History, 1986.

Keefe, Laurence E., Jr. and Dennis Inch. **The Life of a Photograph.** Boston: Focal Press, 1984.

Kyvig, David E., and Myron A. Marty. **Nearby History: Exploring the Past Around You.** Nashville: American Association for State and Local History, 1982.

Lanman, Barry A. and George Mehaffy. "Oral History in the Secondary School Classroom." Pamphlet #2. Los Angeles: Oral History Association, 1989.

Loomis, Ormond H. **Cultural Conservation: The Protection of Cultural Heritage in the United States.** Washington, D.C.: Library of Congress, 1983.

Mercier, Laurie and Madeline Buckendorf. "Using Oral History in Community Projects." Pamphlet #4. Los Angeles: Oral History Association, 1992.

Neuenschwander, John A. "Oral History and the Law." Pamphlet #1. Albuquerque: Oral History Association, 1993.

Purdue, Charles L. Jr., Thomas E. Barden and Robert K. Phillips, eds., **Weevils in the Wheat: Interviews with Virginia Ex-Slaves.** Bloomington: Indiana University Press, 1976, rev.1980.

Reilly, James J. **Care and Identification of 19th-Century Photographic Prints.** Rochester, NY: Eastman Kodak Company, 1986.

Ritchie, Donald A. **Doing Oral History.** Twayne's Oral History Series No. 15. New York: Twayne Publishers, 1995

_____ , ed. "Oral History Evaluation Guidelines." Pamphlet #3. Los Angeles: Oral History Association, 1992. Rev. ed.

Ritzenthaler, Mary Lynn, et al. **Archives and Manuscripts: Administration of Photographic Collections.** Chicago: Society of American Archivists, 1984.

Rosengarten, Theodore. **All God's Dangers: The Life of Nate Shaw.** New York: Knopf, 1974.

Schorzman, Terri A. ed. **A Practical Introduction to Videohistory: The Smithsonian Institution and Alfred P. Sloan Experiment.** Malabar, FL: Krieger Publishing Co., 1993.

_____. "Smithsonian Videohistory Program Symposium," **Technology and Culture**, 30, 118-22, (1989).

Sipe, Dan. "Media and Public History; The Future of Oral History and Moving Images," **Oral History Review**, 19:1-2, 75-87, (1991).

Spradley, James P. **Participant Observation.** New York: Holt, Rinehart and Winston, 1980.

_____. **The Ethnographic Interview.** New York: Holt, Rinehart and Winston, 1979.

_____. and David W. McCurdy. **The Cultural Experience: Ethnography in Complex Society.** Chicago: Science Research Association, 1972.

Suter, John W. **Working with Folk Materials in New York State: A Manual for Folklorists and Archivists.** New York Folklore Society, 1994.

Taylor, David A. **Documenting Maritime Folklife: An Introductory Guide.** Publications of the American Folklife Center, No. 18. Washington, DC: Government Printing Office, 1992.

Thompson, Paul. **The Voice of the Past: Oral History.** Oxford: Oxford University Press, 1978.

Toelken, Barre. **The Dynamics of Folklore.** Boston: Houghton Mifflin Company, 1979.

Weinstein, Robert A. and Larry Booth. **Collection, Use and Care of Historical Photographs**. Nashville: American Association for State and Local History, 1977.

Wilson, Joseph an Lee Udall. **Folk Festivals: A Handbook for Organization and Management.** Knoxville: University of Tennessee Press, 1982.